HIGH LIFE
LOW LIFE

Living with bipolar disorder

LIAM GILDEA

Copyright © Liam Gildea 2021
This book is sold subject to the condition that it shall not, by way of trade or otherwise, be lent, resold, hired out, or otherwise circulated without the publisher's prior consent in any form of binding or cover other than that in which it is published and without a similar condition including this condition being imposed on the subsequent publisher.
The moral right of Liam Gildea has been asserted.
ISBN-13: 9798473522129

This book has not been created to be specific to any individual's or organizations' situation or needs. Every effort has been made to make this book as accurate as possible. This book should serve only as a general guide and not as the ultimate source of subject information. This book contains information that might be dated and is intended only to educate and entertain. The author shall have no liability or responsibility to any person or entity regarding any loss or damage incurred, or alleged to have incurred, directly or indirectly, by the information contained in this book.

CONTENTS

ACKNOWLEDGEMENTS i

INTRODUCTION 1
CHAPTER 1 3
   Depths of despair 3
   Six months earlier: 7
   Welcome to the zoo 7
   Teenage trauma 11
CHAPTER 2 15
   Bipolar II diagnosis and acceptance 15
   What's the difference between mania and hypomania? 19
   The only bipolar in the village 23
   Talkathon 25
   Suicide ideation 29
CHAPTER 3 32
   Fight Club 32
   The Centre 36
   Surviving depressive episodes with no medication 43
   Medication compliance 47
CHAPTER 4 54
   The suspicious walking criminal 54
   Why bother? 58
   Guilt and shame 61
   Media portrayal 63
CHAPTER 5 67
   Online dating 67
   Rachel: America's First Lady 71
   Anger 76
   CBT 80

CHAPTER 6 84
A cocktail of medication 84
The Roscommon Heist 88
Celebrities and Bipolar 92
CHAPTER 7 95
Stigma 95
Low Self-Confidence and Sensitivity 99
The Chase 102
CHAPTER 8 105
Unemployment 105
Employers: the good and the bad 108
Overspending and Peacocking 112
Indecision 117
CHAPTER 9 120
Chicago Town 120
Anxiety 124
Concentration 127
CHAPTER 10 131
2008 Missed flights 131
Lack of Understanding 136
Krakow and the Salt Mines 138
CHAPTER 11 143
Pablo Escobar 143
Grandiosity 148
Selfishness bordering Narcissism 151
Skyfall 155
CHAPTER 12 158
Jacinta the Promiscuous Hen 158
How does Bipolar affect the Brain? 161
Energy 164
Circadian Rhythm and Sleeping pills 167
Stimulus Control Therapy 170

CHAPTER 13 173
Not All Heroes Wear capes... *173*
Bipolar and recurring behaviours *176*
One Flew Over the Cuckoo's Nest *179*
Lightbulb moments *182*
CHAPTER 14 185
Cattle break.. *185*
Alexander the Great... *188*
Toxic People and Recovery *191*
CHAPTER 15 195
Living with someone with bipolar illness *195*
Routine and IPSRT (Interpersonal and Social Rhythm Therapy) *198*
CHAPTER 16 201
Preventing relapses... *201*
Supermarket Sweep.. *205*
Bad Cops... *208*
CHAPTER 17 210
The Nomad.. *210*
Wellness... *215*
Turning the tide *218*
End Game *221*
REFERENCES... 224

ACKNOWLEDGEMENTS

To my family, friends, fiancée Joanne who have been with me in my 20-year battle with bipolar illness. A special thanks to my doctor Diarmuid and all the staff in the Claremorris psychiatric day care centre. Finally, many thanks to my editor Maggie Wood for her dedication and professionalism in helping to bring this book to publication.

INTRODUCTION

In this book I will take you through the past 20 years, living with mental illness. I will recount stories of paralyzing lows to frenzied highs that mark a condition called Bipolar illness. I will be reflecting on the devastation of these episodes leading to troubles with authorities, online dating addiction and culminating in suicide ideation.

This book is not in chronological order and purposely so. There is a sense of madness that comes along with bipolar, there is no structure in one's life. Episodes run into each other and there is no stability. Particularly in periods of elated mood I was jumping from one lunacy to the next. The unstructured style of the book reflects this.

The book hops quickly from one episode to the next. It doesn't have to be read in any particular order, you can dip in and out reading stories as separate entities. I believe reading enough of the stories on their own will give you a good grasp of what living with bipolar is like. I'll look at people who have influenced my perception of life, from online gurus to counsellors to Cognitive Behavioural therapists. I will describe the pain of anxiety to the beautiful feeling of hypomania.

If you are living with bipolar illness or have a family member with the illness it's my hope that this book is of some help. I was in and out of a psychiatric day care centre for 6 years and have picked up invaluable information from the healthcare professionals. I try to relay this knowledge at all opportunities in this book. I hope you learn from my mistakes and appreciate the importance of getting professional help that'll lead to a proper diagnosis. I hope you can get beyond stigma, accept your illness, and move forward to being the best you.

Whilst living with a mental health condition can be extremely difficult it can be a great teacher. It's my earnest hope that by the end of the book you will realise that no mental illness defines you as a person. You're on the cusp of a life worth living, it's just a matter of making the next right step.

CHAPTER 1

Depths of despair

It's a Tuesday evening in mid-April 2013. The Boston Marathon bombing was the previous day, so April 15th is etched into my mind. I'm on my way home from Galway. The journey is mostly a blur. I recall the teeming rain beating on my windscreen. My mind is dangerously absent. I am suicidal. I haven't slept or ate right in weeks. I weigh eight stone. I'm frail and gaunt looking. All I want is to be dead, nothing else. I'm hoping a lorry will veer across and take me out of my misery. It would be such a relief.

I stop off in Tuam to meet my cousin. I'm not able to articulate the depths of my despair. I find it very difficult to structure basic sentences. I can tell he's worried that he's never seen me at such a low ebb. I'm in tears. He mentions that maybe hospitalisation would be a good intervention due to the seriousness of the situation. At this stage, these lows were happening for 14 years. The lows lasted anything from 6 to 18 months. Earlier in the day my GP had called me at work to see how I was doing. He's very concerned. I have to meet him first thing on Wednesday morning. I just have the energy to tell my cousin about the appointment.

I continue the drive home devoid of hope. My parents are wondering what I'm doing home mid-week. I briefly fill them in. I don't mention suicide ideation, just that I'm low. I have family in Boston, my mother tells me that there are all safe and well. I turn on the TV. Barcelona are playing Bayern Munich in a champion's league semi-final. Even if the game were across the garden, I wouldn't go over to see it. I wonder why I ever had any interest in sport. It just seems so inane. The suicidal thoughts are incessant.

I go to bed early. I stare at the ceiling all night. The house is eerily quiet. I feel like a small child with no control over my life. "I am just waiting for someone to give me some guidance". I pray to God to die overnight. I can't face another day of this hell. I get up and head into my GP for 9am. I pack a bag just in case. He has known me for 4 years. He's seen me severely depressed before but never at this magnitude. I tell him that I have no interest in living and if an opportunity arose, I'd take my own life.

For my own safety he refers me to A&E. He tells me there's a psychiatric day care centre in Claremorris, the town next to me. If he puts me on a referral list, I would be up to two months waiting. We both know

I'll be dead if the intervention isn't by the latest Friday. If I go through A&E, they will be able to fast track me into the clinic by tomorrow.

I head for Castlebar hospital a 40-minute journey. I daydream of paying some hitman to put a bullet in my head. I was suicidal but didn't have the clarity of thought on how to actually kill myself. I'm sitting in A&E staring into the abyss. It's quiet, there's four others waiting. How the hell did I end up here? What have I done to deserve this? I am ashamed. Life was supposed to be cherished and all I want is to be dead. I am in my late 20s; in my prime, how am I suicidal? I have a job, a girlfriend and am living with a few mates in Galway. What have I to be depressed about?

I'm about an hour waiting. A nurse calls me in wondering what's going on. She says I look tired and asked had I been sleeping. "Not for weeks" I said. She continues to probe. She eventually asks - am I suicidal? I lie. I told her I was having fleeting suicidal thoughts but have no intent of killing myself. She is happy enough to let me go home.

She prescribes me a few sleeping pills and tells me that I would get a call from the psychiatric day care centre the following day. That night I took 2 tablets as prescribed.

I sleep a few hours but wake at 5am the next morning. One of the issues with sleeping pills, is once you wake there is no returning to sleep. I feel like a zombie, just completely out of it. I wait for the call which didn't come till afternoon. I hear visitors coming to the door around 11am. I can't face them. I stay in my room. The thought of talking to anyone is nauseating. I don't know what lays before me. I haven't even heard of this day care centre. I would become very familiar with this place over the next 6 years. It didn't seem it at the time, but this episode would prove the first pivotal step in a long recovery.

Six months earlier:

Welcome to the zoo

October 2012 - I was rocketing, and my behaviour was becoming more and more erratic. I felt fantastic. My online dating exploits were going to go outside Connaught. I was heading for Tullamore in Offaly on a Thursday evening. It was a good 90 minutes' drive. There was excitement running through my veins. I had just been chatting to this woman online for a day. She asked me up for an overnight stay. It seemed normal to me at the time to head two hours up the country for a hook up. When I was high, I was very impulsive. I never weighed up the pros and the cons of any situation. For a sane mind, heading to Offaly to meet a random stranger with work the next morning was bizarre to say the least

I arrived up and met this girl at The Brewery Tap right in the middle of the town. It was relatively quiet with a few auld fellas drinking pints of Guinness at the bar. Nicola had told me she was also sitting at the bar. I could see her blonde hair as I approached the counter. You never really knew whether the woman you were meeting resembled the photo of the woman on the online dating platform, thankfully on this occasion she did. We had an awkward hug type embrace. She ordered me a drink without even asking,

"Finbar, can I get two Tullamore Dews". I'm not a fan of whiskey but it would have been rude to say no. I felt like an American tourist.

I could tell the locals were weighing me up, it was that type of bar. Anyone outside of the town would stand out. Before we had started a proper conversation two women came into the pub and approached the bar. Nicola introduced me to her two sisters. We shook hands.

She didn't tell me that her two sisters would be joining us. Nicola suggested we grabbed a table. These women were fierce country. The main conversation centred around how their two brothers joined thousands of farmers marching through Dublin city protesting at the farmer cuts on the Tuesday. Finally, the conversation turned to me. A few probing questions, what did I do, where was I from. A bit of banter about the football. At no stage did Nicola mention to our company where she met me. It was the elephant in the room. We didn't have much in common. It never veered beyond chit chat. We had a couple of whiskeys drank at this stage.

Nicola was a vet and unsurprisingly an animal lover. I'm a dog lover myself so finally the conversation began to flow. Once the two sisters left us, shortly after 11pm we headed back to her place. She lived in a country mansion. The first thing that struck me was her winding stairs in the middle of the hall. I walked further into the house there was an unusual smell, quite overpowering. Here is where this date took a turn for the worse.

She gave me a tour of the house. I was about to find out to what extent her affection of animals went. In the first room were two piglets. How weird, I thought. The next room a monkey and two parrots. This was a pet farm. She even had a four-year-old Shetland pony. She had converted a box room to a shed full of straw. The final room was normal, no animals in sight or that's what I thought. What do you think of my iguana? I said sure that's only a toy on your window. Next thing the fella jumped three feet.

As we walked up the steps, I met her golden Labrador, he had free rein. We got into bed. I had to ask.

Do animals ever sleep with you?

Usually just my dog rusty. At the weekends, the monkey hops in.

O for the love of God. It was one long night, I didn't sleep a wink. She offered to cook 7am breakfast, but at that stage I was running late for work. I took the easy option and left quickly. I put the foot down and haven't been back to Offaly since. If someone else had told me that story I'd have thought along the lines of "never let the truth ruin a good story". However, that's how the evening played out.

This would really sum up my life and my illness for the guts of a decade. I would go from strange gratifying behaviour to the pits of despair in the matter of 5 months.

Teenage trauma

As is typical for a mental illness my mood disorder arrived in the teenage years. My first depressive episode was in 1999 when I turned 16.

I returned to school in September 1999 to begin 4th year. From the second I woke in the morning I felt drained. I felt weighed down by emotional turmoil, that at the time I just thought was life itself. I started to slowly withdraw from my circle of friends. I didn't feel I had anything to say that was worthwhile. The guy who cracked jokes all day last year was long gone. Trying to focus on class was nearly impossible. I would be falling asleep in class even though I had had 10 hours sleep the night before.

Back in 1999 nobody spoke of depression. I had never even heard of the word. There were no mental health wellbeing days back then. My skin started flaring up with acne and psoriasis. One of the cruel ironies of being a teenager, the time you're most self-conscious is when acne arrives. I blamed my skin for my bad mood. I tried to rationalise it. There had to be some external cause for this horrible empty feeling. For most teenagers it was part of life to have skin problems. They would pass in due course. It made most kids subconscious but didn't have any detrimental effect on their lives. This wasn't the case for me. I felt my skin looked dreadful and I despised the way I looked.

I always felt my friends were judging me. I imagined they were all talking about my skin whilst sniggering. My gang of friends for the most part had perfect skin. I envied them. When I spoke, I covered my face with my hand. A few months later, I overheard two of my friends saying, how I always covered my chin whilst speaking. This made me even more subconscious. It began to become an obsession. I could look at the mirror 30 times a day. My focus was solely on my skin. I chose to ignore the fact I was very underweight and frail. My behaviour was borne out of anxiety and poor self-esteem. Low self-confidence would stay with me for the next two decades.

At no stage of the day did I feel well within myself. When I was eating, I had a knot in my stomach from worries. I was eating but due to sheer anxiety I don't think my body was absorbing the nutrition it needed. My anxiety heightened as the months passed by

I knew deep down it wasn't normal to be this unhappy. My grades plummeted dramatically. In retrospect the slide had begun in the junior cert year. That year such was my level of excitement it led to lack of concentration, the first signs of an elated mood.

As time passed by, to protect myself from not fitting in at school, occasionally I played the comedian in class. It was effectively a mask. Unknown to myself I had created a separate character to cover up my mental illness. I would continue this façade for years to come. I didn't want to be different; nobody does as a teenager. In 2013, 14 years later I would realise, wearing the mask took more energy out of my feeble body than the depression itself.

When I went home my mood was constantly low. I would withdraw from my family. Some weeks I was rapid cycling, considerably changing mood twice in one day. I think I fooled my teachers and classmates to thinking I was a normal enough teenager, just a little moody. The reality was I hated myself. I longed to be someone else.

I was always well liked. On the few Saturday nights I went out I would use my sense of humour to disguise my social anxiety. With girls now in the equation I tried extra hard to keep up the façade. The few bottles of Bacardi Breezer helped. I had good friends, they involved me as much as possible in the crack. However, that inferior feeling was always there

I put my depression down to being a moody teenager. It was very hard to detect that there were any signs of mental illness. All teenagers were moody. One teacher was clued in. She saw my decline. She questioned me as to whether I was doing extra work on the farm at home. We didn't have a farm. She commented that I looked very tired. I believe that she knew I was depressed but didn't want to probe any further. I thought I would be somehow fixed when I went to college. This wouldn't be the case. Little did I know, 20 years of hell awaited.

CHAPTER 2

Bipolar II diagnosis and acceptance

On the face of it, my diagnosis looked very clear cut. I had severe depression. Any checklist of symptoms I looked at online, I met all the criteria for that diagnosis. From insomnia to no appetite, feelings of despair, lack of energy and concentration, to thoughts of suicide. They were the main symptoms of the condition and I had them all.

Bipolar disorder is a brain disorder that causes unusual shifts in mood, energy, activities, and the ability to carry out daily tasks. According to the National Institution of Mental Health there are 27 million people world-wide, excluding children, who have bipolarity. It affects both men and women equally. People suffering from the illness can't directly alter brain chemistry any more than a person with diabetes can regulate insulin level through willpower alone (Preston and Fast, 2006). Bipolar disorder has a relatively early age of onset, with the peak age of onset being 15-19 years old. Most experts agree that the causes range from genetics to a person's environment, the average being 70% genetic and 30% environment. This may not be the case for every individual. For some it might be 40% genetic and 60% environmental or other variables (McKeon, 2018.)

In 1980 the name bipolar disorder was adopted to replace the older term manic depression. One of the difficulties in getting a bipolar diagnosis is that there is no brain scan that can diagnose the illness. There is no bipolar gene. There is no clear test. It is estimated that over 50% of people with the condition never get diagnosed. A large retrospective study of patients with bipolar disorder reported that there was an average of 5-10 years' delay from a person's first recollected mood episode to receiving a diagnosis of bipolar disorder (O'Carroll, 2013). It is estimated that the average patient will have 10 bipolar episodes in their lifetime. A person who has bipolar is 15-20 times more likely to commit suicide than the general population.

In April 2013 I finally got a diagnosis of bipolar II. My doctor had hinted at a bipolar illness two years previously. I had a very vague understanding of bipolar illness. I understood at a basic level that there were highs and lows. My nurse had told me, that the second I walked into the day care centre she had sussed that I was bipolar II. Thirty years' experience gives that natural insight.

My doctor had mentioned that a bipolar illness was treated with different medication than depression. The tablets were known as mood stabilisers. The issue with me for years, was that I would only present myself to my doctor when I was clinically depressed. I would never inform him that I had been on a high for a few months previously, although for years I had no awareness of my elated mood. So, it appeared mine was a case of depression only. I had been treated accordingly.

I was to learn that there were two main types of bipolar illness, bipolar I and bipolar II. I would fall under the bipolar II spectrum. There is another strain of bipolarity which isn't as common called Cyclothymia. This is where there are mild periods of depression (don't qualify as major depressive episodes) alternating with periods of elated mood that are very mild on the spectrum. It is regrettably referenced as 'bipolar lite' even though the illness can cause severe impairment.

All sufferers of bipolar I and II will suffer with severe depression. The main difference between the two types of bipolar come in the severity of the highs. Bipolar type II highs are labelled hypomania, whilst bipolar type I highs are labelled manic. This is an important distinction which I will examine in detail shortly. It is something I am asked regularly, is bipolar

II a milder version of bipolar I? This is an assumption that is inherently risky. Several studies show that there is a higher suicide rate for people who have bipolar II (Parker, 2019).

Hypomania is a mood state characterized by persistent disinhibition and mood elevation, also described as euphoria. On a conscious level it didn't take me too long to get an understanding of the illness. On a sub conscious level, I struggled to accept the disorder. It would take me five years to get to a level of full acceptance. From talking to other sufferers, they also struggled to accept that they had the condition. The nurse told me I would be on medication for the rest of my life. This didn't sit well with me at all. I was 30 years of age, too young to have a serious mental illness. In the following few years, I would come off medication twice by my own accord. On both occasions it would prove nearly fatal. On reflection, this was born out of not being able to fully accept the illness.

What's the difference between mania and hypomania?

The key difference between bipolar I and bipolar II is the level of mania experienced by the sufferer. The word mania is derived from a Greek word which means "speeded up". (McKeon, 2018). Depression exists in both illnesses. The word depression is derived from the Greek word to slow down. The symptoms of mania and hypomania are somewhat similar. Hypomania and mania are periods of overactive and excited behaviour that have a significant impact on your day-to-day life (Warin, 2016). Those of mania are more intense. In general terms, mania escalates to the point of hospitalisation. For those with a bipolar II condition, the individual is never psychotic when they're high or depressed. In my view, that's the key distinguishing feature. Unlike hypomanic episodes, manic episodes can lead to serious consequences. With mania, you may also have a break from reality. Psychotic symptoms can include:

- visual or auditory hallucinations
- delusional thoughts
- paranoid thoughts.

I witnessed one person going through a full-blown

manic episode. It was frightening. At the time it wasn't something I could comprehend. She had lost touch with reality. It was 16 years ago so it was long before I knew I had a similar illness. There were a few people present, none of us had any knowledge of bipolarity. We were trying to rationalise what had happened. If it's one thing I now know about bipolar, it's no more rational than Parkinson's disease. Looking back, she displayed two of the main psychotic symptoms.

Delusional thoughts were very evident. She believed she lived in Buckingham Palace with the Queen and was a millionaire. She became paranoid, feeling all the neighbours were talking about him and were full of jealously. Aggression was also present. Looking back, I can relate to her anger and aggression, but not at that level. Unfortunately, she had to be hospitalized as she was becoming a danger to herself and others. She never got treatment for her disorder. I don't believe she was ever aware she had an illness. One of the reasons the episode was so severe, was that she never was on any medication. It was a ticking bomb waiting to happen

Looking back, the fact it's a very treatable condition fills me with sadness. It could have all been prevented. Perhaps she knew deep down there was something not right. Such was the level of stigma back then, who could she talk to?

The Diagnostic and Statistical Manual of mental disorders states that one of the things that differs is the minimum time a manic episode must last to be diagnosed as bipolar I. The symptoms must last one week for mania, four days for hypomania. Once you have a bipolar I diagnosis it stays that way even if in future episodes you experience are hypomanic. On the other hand, if you have a bipolar II diagnoses and down the road you have a manic episode your condition is upgraded to bipolar I. Studies suggest there's a 17% chance that if a person is diagnosed with bipolar type II, that they will have a manic episode and move to bipolar I (Lauren et al, 2011).

On average, people with bipolar disorder spend more time experiencing depressive symptoms than manic symptoms. This is particularly the case in bipolar II disorder. In one study, the ratio of time depressed to hypomania was 37:1 compared with 3:1 in bipolar I disorder (Judd, 2002). Twelve percent of people who have unipolar depression have a hypomanic episode at some stage in their life. If this happens the diagnosis changes from major depressive order to bipolar II disorder, even if it's just one hypomanic episode. It will never go back to being diagnosed as major depressive order.

The treatment and medication for strains of the illness are much the same. The course of the illness is different. People with bipolar I can have back-to-back manic episodes with very few depressive episodes. People with bipolar II can have longer and more frequent depressive episodes. Bipolar disease is lifelong and can have a massive impact on your life. However, with treatment, it can be well managed, and you can live a life as rich and fulfilling as anyone else.

The only bipolar in the village

There was a programme on the BBC in the early noughties called Little Britain. Written by comedian David Walliams, there was a great Welsh character called Daffyd in it. He was the only gay in the village which he reiterated at every opportunity. He also maintained that everyone in the village was homophobic. Of course, this wasn't the case. Nobody had any issue with his sexuality. On several occasions there were more than himself sitting in the bar who was gay, but he chose to ignore this.

In 2013 when I got the official bipolar diagnosis, I felt like the only bipolar person in Ballyhaunis. I didn't know one person who had this diagnosis. In my head this further added to the stigma. When I checked out the number of sufferers In Ireland, 40,000 people had a diagnosis of bipolar illness. That worked out per capita of 1/120. Jesus, like what were the chances of getting landed with the disorder. Yet here I was at 30 years of age being dealt this horrid illness. I always felt people were talking about me behind my back. I noticed a lot of people were very awkward around me. Some people would leave the room if there were only the two of us.

There was no actual evidence that people were talking about me in a negative manner. Making assumptions on what other people are thinking is fraught with difficulty. When we assume what someone else thinks this is often coloured by our own issues. Projection is a defence mechanism where you project your own thoughts on to someone else and believe that's what the other person is thinking (Marks, 2019).

Perhaps they understood elements of the condition better than I thought. Like Daffyd, my perception of people thinking I was strange was an assumption. As the years passed, I grew to know a lot of people locally who suffered with depression. They may not have had any experience of the hypomanic side of the illness, but they certainly knew all about depression and could relate to it.

Talkathon

In December 2008, five years before an official diagnosis was made, I was experiencing textbook hypomanic symptoms. I would discover over time that one of the earliest signs of a hypomanic episode for me, was rapid speech. This is a common symptom for people with a bipolar illness. Rapid speech differs from ordinary talkativeness. A noticeable change in a person's usual manner of speaking is evident. The individual speaks at a rapid and sometimes frantic speed. The pace makes it difficult for people listening to make sense of what is being said. Pressured speech can be jumbled and difficult to understand, as the person speaking may not stop at appropriate points. It manifests as a compelling, virtually irresistible desire to talk (Purse 2019).

The conversation would begin normally enough with brief exchanges. If you asked me my opinion on something, I could easily talk for 30 minutes without a breath. I wouldn't give you any chance to join in on the conversation. It was effectively a one-way conversation. I had an extreme need to share my thoughts and ideas. When you would eventually break my constant monologue, I'd give you a 20 second window, before I started another rant.

My mind was racing 100 miles an hour. I imagine I

was difficult to understand. I was always jumping between topics at an incredible speed. I could discuss five different topics in a few minutes. None of the subjects would be related. I was very incoherent.

I had a flight of ideas. I had no control over my speech. For years I wasn't aware of this early sign that I was quickly going up through the gears. I lost all judgement of when it was appropriate to have a full-blown conversation. I got pulled up by a few managers at work who told me to shut up. I didn't take their advice on board and kept talking. They had no right to tell me I couldn't talk. My topic of choice tended to be very inappropriate for any workplace.

Like a small child I spoke without a filter. Unlike most people, I didn't put my thoughts through the sieve of reflection. I didn't have the capacity to consider whether what I was planning on saying was appropriate or not. I spoke with honesty but to the extreme. I couldn't fathom out why my colleagues wouldn't converse in a familiar fashion. In my mind their conversation was so mundane. It didn't help matters that I was extremely loud. As is common these days most offices are open plan. I'm sure me chirping away for an hour at 9am on a Monday morning went down a treat. I can only imagine how infuriating it would be to have someone talking at you rather than talking to you. It must have come across as extreme arrogance.

In December 2008 I had decided to switch from a ready-to- go to a bill phone. I had so much to say. It was an inconvenience for my credit to run out. I'll never forget the day I called O2 to see what my monthly balance was. I was expecting the bill to be around 100 euro. I had spent 19 hours on the phone talking that first week in December. The bill was €527. I nearly dropped. I was working full time so I'm not sure how I managed to fit in all those hours of conversation. As I was blowing my money on other things, I didn't have that cash to spare.

At the time it seemed perfectly normal to ring the phone company and demand that they take a few hundred euros off the bill as I was a loyal customer. The worst thing was that if I had picked the right phone plan, I could have had unlimited calls for €60. This was a textbook symptom of bipolar, not thinking a decision through, not carrying out any research and acting completely on impulse.

Even now looking back I question how I managed to lose the ability of controlling my level of speech. At the time, the thought never occurred to me that this was unusual behaviour. I was oblivious to it all. Most of the calls were late at night. I had the urge to call people I hadn't seen in years. I remember scrolling through my contacts alphabetically. It was as if I was cold calling except I had nothing to sell. God knows how anyone listened. I had called a few ex-girlfriends and those calls lasted to close to two hours so that would have made up six of the 19 hours. The other 13 hours is anyone's guess.

Over the past 20 years, anytime I experienced rapid speech, a few months later without fail I ended up being severely depressed. When I followed my typical cycle of returning to a deep depression, I had to pay the money I owed, by 12 instalment payments. My contract was up at work in February, and I was let go. Out of my dole I had to pay €44 a week to my phone company. What an idiot I had been.

With depression you tend not to be able to make decisions at all, in a hypomanic episode you would make decisions, but they would invariably turn out to be the wrong ones. So, the net effect was the same. You would have been as well off if you didn't make the decision at all. You'd have thought I'd have learned a costly lesson. A couple of years later I ran up a €200 phone bill. The penny finally dropped after that to watch my phone usage.

Pressured speech can be one of the more difficult symptoms of bipolar disorder. This is because it's difficult to control or stop when it happens. It can also have wide-ranging repercussions or complications in all areas of life.

Suicide ideation

For most people, the idea that a person would want to be dead is a frightening thought and one that is difficult to comprehend. What is suicide ideation? It's thoughts of wanting to be dead, which vary from fleeting thoughts to extensive thoughts of detailed planning or a complete preoccupation with self-destruction. It does not include the final act of suicide (Brazier 2018). Due to the severity of depression experienced by a person with bipolar disorder, thoughts of death are usually present. At the outset it is important to note that most people who have suicide ideation don't go on to take their own life.

If I were to look back at a photo that was taken in the past 15 years I'd know by my appearance, whether I was experiencing suicide ideation. Extremely low weight and a gaunt appearance were the biggest physical indicators.

There are two kinds of suicidal ideation: passive and active. Passive suicidal ideation occurs when you wish you were dead or that you could die. However, you don't actually have any plans to commit suicide. Active suicidal ideation, on the other hand, is not only thinking about it but having the intent to commit suicide, including planning how to do it.

My suicidal thoughts in the main would be

categorised as being in the passive category. They were present at every waking moments of the day. I would take a drive to a seaside location and park up. I'd go to a place like Rinville in Galway. I would walk out to the edge of the water. I'd long to jump in but didn't have the courage. On reflection, this really was a sign that somewhere buried in my subconscious I wanted to live.

In the middle of my last depressive episode in 2018 I was driving home from work. I was working in a multinational in Athlone. I hated working there, but such was the severity of my illness I hated everything. It was a very wet evening. I came off the motorway way too fast approaching a dangerous slip off. Suddenly, I lost control of the car. The immediate thought I had was not fear but one of relief. This could be the answer to my prayers. I let the action run its course, but it wasn't to be. I ended up in the ditch but there was no damage done to me or the car. A golden opportunity had passed. If only I was going 30km quicker. My agonizing mental torture could have been over.

Passive suicide ideation is still high risk. Some clinicians think that it is not useful to distinguish active and passive ideation. I think their point is, that people shouldn't disregard passive ideation as something that isn't acutely serious. The risk of suicide for people with bipolar is extreme. It is estimated that 15% of people with bipolar take their own lives. In comparison, the rest of the population have a suicide rate of 1.4% (World Health Organization, 2016).

CHAPTER 3

Fight Club

In July 2010 I was nearing the end of a hypomanic episode. I was entering the argumentative stage. I could turn on anyone for no apparent reason. It was almost like I attracted other angry people. Bipolar rage is a side of the disorder that has long passed under the radar screen. Mania tends to trigger aggressive emotions and anger. For many this uncontrolled anger has destroyed their marriages, families, and personal relationships. It has ruined their careers and left them emotionally isolated.

A mate John and I decided to head down to Castlebar for a night out. It was quiet for a Saturday night, but so were all towns in Mayo. The recession had ripped them apart. We arrived down at 9pm and headed to Rocky's, a pub in the middle of the town. We stood away from the bar as there were no stools available. I felt a little paranoid, that people were looking at me. Castlebar is one of those towns where the locals rule the roost. Any stranger from outside the town is noticed quickly. There were a couple of women standing beside us. I tried to chat up one of them but to no avail. My tone of voice was narky, and my conversation was a bit intense.

We hit the Captain Morgan's and Coke around 10pm. I rarely drank shorts. I was getting messy. We walked down to the Front Lounge, a nightclub down the road, after midnight. Once the fresh air caught me the captain Morgan's hit me like a train. It was a small club, so it was packed. The same people were standing at the bar that were there four years ago. That was one of the few things that I remember. We left early enough and hit for Supermac's for a burger.

After pissing about in there for 20 minutes we hit down the town. I had got a bottle of water to sober me up. I was in one of those moods where I didn't give a toss about anything. When I was like that I was never far from trouble. I almost revelled in it. As we walked down the street a boy racer drove towards us in a souped-up Honda Civic. I flung the bottle of water as hard as I could at the passenger side window. This wouldn't have been my brightest idea. The hand brake was pulled up and two young fellas leapt out of the car. John stopped one of them. The other guy went straight for me. I was too pissed to put up a fight. He knocked me out. He had hit me a dig right in the lip. It was no more than I deserved.

They drove off John picked me up. Great! a busted

lip. It was late. At this stage there were no taxis. The only choice was to sleep in my car. As I walked towards the car, I realised I had left my iPhone in Supermac's. I ran back. It was gone. Honest to God could this night get any worse... Of course, it could.

We headed back to the car to sleep for the night. Shortly after five in the morning there was a knock on my window, two Gardaí. I rolled down the window.

What are ye doing lads?

We were down for a few drinks and missed the taxis, so we have to sleep in my car.

Why would you come down to this hole for a night out?

My lip was busted. This was spotted. A barrage of questions. I had been physically assaulted, but the guard said I had only myself to blame. Fair enough, piss off and let me go to sleep.

Can you get out of the car please?

At the time I had a year 2000 Mazda 323 and the electrics were after going. I couldn't get out my side of the car. The only option was to get out the passenger side.

Sorry guard I can't.

Okay open the boot.

Sorry guard I can't the electrics are gone.

Right, I'm going to confiscate this car on the

suspicion that your vehicle contains drugs.

What the hell, that escalated quickly.

Hold on hold on, John get out I need to get out of the car.

So, I'm arguing with the guard that I have never taken or sold drugs. I'm not El Chapo. She wasn't budging. The car was going to be taken...

O hold on I can get into my boot.

I had forgotten I could pull the back seats out so you could see into the boot. There were no drugs in the car.

She went back to her car and put my car's registration into her Pulse system... Somehow my car wasn't registered to myself. It was under some Polish guy's name. Obviously, the guy I bought the car off. Christ! Now she wanted to confiscate the car because it was a stolen vehicle.

I talked her round. My insurance disk on my window was from my previous car. My car was insured but god knows what I did with the new disk. I had to present myself in Ballyhaunis garda station with all my paperwork on the following Monday or she'd put a warrant out for my arrest. The guards headed off. John was pissing himself laughing. A busted lip, a stolen iPhone, and my car nearly being confiscated. I had had better nights.

The Centre

In April 2013 I arrived in this day care centre, severely depressed. This would be a place I would frequent for the next six years. Had I been aware of that, it would have been very hard to accept. Just as well I couldn't see into the future. Three trips to hell awaited.

This was an acute psychiatric day care centre, which was a better option I felt, than being admitted to a mental health hospital. I had heard good and bad stories about the nearest hospital. Some would speak about it positively, citing the level of care and good food. Others would tell me stories about their cigarettes being stolen and the premises being depressing. I was thankful that my psychiatrist decided that it would damage my already low self-esteem to be admitted.

It was a strange place, I thought. It was a four-bedroom house laid out in a similar fashion to a normal house. On the right was the secretary's office. On the left was the doctor's room. The last two rooms were a patient's kitchen and a waiting room. Upstairs were an art room, staff kitchen and two consultancy rooms.

At my worst I would spend most of the day in the waiting room looking out the window. I hadn't the energy to talk to anyone bar my nurse. I would have a six-month period of being there nearly every day except weekends for my first stint in 2013. I was high risk. I was safer there.

I was monosyllabic for the first two months. The psychiatrist struggled to get much out of me on our bi-weekly appointments. First off, I had to get a diagnosis. Secondly, I had to get my sleep and appetite back to some normality.

So, what type of people did I meet there? There were generally up to 10 patients coming and going throughout the day. What struck me was how it represented the whole fabric of society, from teenagers to middle age to the old. It was split evenly between male and female patients. As I got to know a few of the patients they spoke about what careers they were in, from engineers to teachers to farmers to bus drivers to college students to old age pensioners. These were normal people who happened to be struggling with mental illness. I would meet people who'd have known me from home to people I went to school with 20 years ago. Initially I was embarrassed and the feeling I got, so were they. Overtime this embarrassment would disappear. What use did it serve? None.

I made a few friends. The fact that there were a few young people there as well didn't make me feel quite as bad. I grew comfort from the fact that there were other people in the same boat as me. Some of us were more ill than others. In a future depressive episode, I would easily have been the most depressed person there. When I was well, the psychiatrist informed me of that fact. She said I had been the most depressed person she had seen in years. She said I looked like someone who had the early onset of Parkinson's disease, such was my mask like face.

If my concentration was good enough, I could read the paper. In the afternoon I would go for some lunch. It provided some structure in the day. There was a great initiative ran by the HSE where they subsidised your lunch. You could get a meal in one of the bars in town for two euro. It was a great help as I was on a social welfare payment. As the illness had ravaged me to my bones my body really needed the nutrition of a proper meal. At the beginning I found it very difficult to eat a big dinner. All food tasted very bland, like I was eating cardboard. As the months passed by, I began to enjoy the food. This was a very early indicator that I was making progress in my recovery. I would gradually get myself back to a somewhat normal weight. I had a stone of weight back on in the space of three months. Even at that I was still underweight at nine stone.

There were days when you knew who didn't want to converse. 2013 happened to be a beautiful summer, there was a nice garden table out the back. When the sun was out, I tended to spend some time sunning myself. When I was there daily my body and mind had succumbed to this horrible illness. I would be seen daily by one of the nurses and every second week by the psychiatrist. Some days I was able to take in what the medical staff were saying. Other days, I was absent minded trying to think of an easy way to take my own life

I was never under any illusion as to how serious it was to be going to a psychiatric unit daily. I would be brutally reminded of the sheer pain some of the patients were in. Over the five years I was there, two guys whom I had grown to know quite well took their own lives. Both had family. It was a tragedy for all involved. Looking back, it could easily have been me. I can recall some weeks of those years in that centre but mostly it's a blur. In ways I'm glad I can't remember those awful times.

A lot of people close to me questioned why I wouldn't go for private treatment. I had heard of one man locally who attended Saint John of God's private service in Dublin with great success. I was getting excellent treatment daily. I didn't feel it would be worthwhile to change ship. Besides, I didn't have the energy to start explaining my illness to another clinic. So, what made this service so good? In most services you were lucky to get a 15 minutes' consultation with a psychiatrist once every three months. Here, the focus was on the level of care the service user was receiving. The sessions weren't rushed. My appointments could last anything ranging from one to two hours. I felt comfortable to say "I wish I was dead" without judgement.

At the beginning it was mostly about the medication I would have to take for the foreseeable future. I focused on trying to increase the number of hours I slept. The nurse linked in with the psychiatrist once a week to give them an update on my progress. This was of paramount importance as there was no guarantee I would see the same psychiatrist every fortnight. It saved me from explaining the whole story about my mental illness.

As the months passed the focus shifted to talk therapy. Once I had regained control of the illness, I was able to partake in short sessions at first. They worked on my confidence and self-esteem. They teased out my value system. We managed to get to the bottom of why I never felt good enough. They taught me how to accept my bipolar diagnosis. And that once under control I could live a fulfilling life. Most of all they provided hope for my future.

At all times, the service user needs were put first. At times, it wasn't advice I wanted to hear, particularly in 2015 after my first relapse, due to not complying with medication. I was told in no uncertain times by my nurse, that poor decision making on my behalf was the main contributory factor to my relapse. Two psychiatrists I saw in the next six weeks echoed this sentiment. I was over complicating the solution. In simple terms, all evidence suggested that when I took my medication as prescribed, I was well able to have a normal life. As one psychiatrist put it to me if I wasn't going to take ownership of my condition why should he be bothered getting me well.

It was never a tick the box exercise with a few generic questions. You could tell that the patient experience was what mattered the most to the nurses. The lasting effect of the talk therapy was teaching me how to take responsibility for my own illness. No amount of treatment would suffice if day to day I was making careless decisions.

I was fortunate I wasn't born in any of the neighbouring counties as this level of service is not available. According to the National Office for suicide prevention annual report, between the years 2004-2016 Roscommon had the second highest suicide rate in the country. I have no doubt there is a correlation here with the level of mental health services available to people. I firmly believe without the service I received, I'd be long dead.

As I write we are in the middle of the COVID-19 pandemic. The experts suggest that the final wave will be a mental health pandemic. With a recession looming there will inevitably be cuts in mental health funding. The trickle-down effect of this, for the day care centre I attended is staff cuts. It will be difficult for the level of service that I received to be replicated for the service users if one staff member's workload has doubled.

I often think if COVID-19 had arrived in 2013 and I was limited to phone consultations, it's hard to imagine I'd have pulled through.

Surviving depressive episodes with no medication

In the early noughties I didn't know one person who was on anti-depressants. Not once did I remotely think there could be a medication out there that could help me with my issues. I never explored treatment options for depression. I was adamant that I didn't have an illness. It was just a stage that I was going through in my life, and I'd eventually get past

My problems, I believed, stemmed from acne and stress at work or in college. If I could solve those issues, life would be a breeze. So, I went through these episodes for the first 10 years without any medication or talk therapy. I never confided in anyone that I wasn't feeling well. I have a few close friends; it said a lot, how stigmatized I felt that I didn't share it with any of them for over 10 years

In college the depression was at a more moderate level. I suffered badly with low confidence and anxiety for a lot of those years. I had a sense that I wasn't well but didn't know how to correct it. I lived in hope that it would eventually pass. A few weeks before the exams I was able to focus and do enough to pass the year.

After I finished college, I went through four horrific

years between the years 2005 to 2009. The first thing that comes to mind when I think of those episodes is the incessant suicidal thoughts. My anxiety had become unbearable. I felt and looked like death. My insomnia was at its worst. I could go days without sleeping. Looking back, the idea of not taking medication to even help me sleep was irrational.

At the time I just wanted to go to bed to get away from life. In one way, I almost liked not sleeping. I knew if I fell asleep, the next time I woke up I would have to face the world again. Deep down during a nasty episode in particular in 2005 I knew that there was something not right. Such was the shame I felt I didn't want to go to my GP. I eventually went in January 2006. I told him I was being bullied at work and I hadn't been feeling well. The word depression was never mentioned. I had only filled him in on a bit of the story. We ran blood tests which came back clean. On the face of it there was nothing wrong with me.

In 2008 one of the lads I lived with Googled some of my symptoms. I was experiencing all the symptoms that were associated with depression. Even then I was in denial. There was some information saying that thyroid disease can cause depression (Nippoldt, 2020). I had lost a lot of weight and maybe this was the reason for feeling so low.

I went to a doctor who wasn't my own GP in Castlebar. I asked him to check if my thyroid was underactive. A week later he got the results back. Of course, my thyroid was completely fine. Now there was no other explanation, only that I was suffering with severe depression. I wasn't overly gone on this doctor which didn't help the case. He was very abrupt. He hadn't an ounce of empathy in his bones. After a three minutes' consultation, he took out a book and started searching through the pages. I asked him what he was looking for. He told me he was looking through anti-depressant medications; to see could he find one that was suitable. I stopped him. I didn't want to take medication. He slammed the book and said there was nothing else he could do so. He didn't give me any alternative options so that was that.

I would continue to muddle through the remainder of this depressive episode. I endured so much unnecessary hardship. Now, albeit I would have been treated for the wrong illness, which would have ended up in a medicated hypomanic episode, at least I would have got relief from some of my symptoms. In 2008 it would be the last occasion I would go through a depressive episode, without the intervention of anti-depressants.

It would be May 2009 before I got a diagnosis of depression. I walked into the surgery very sheepishly. How was I going to explain my ailments when there were no physical signs, I was ill. Looking back, I realize now that there were physical signs. My withered body bore all the hallmarks of a severe depressive episode. I said very little, only that I felt very low and anxious. I was diagnosed with depression and general anxiety disorder. I was prescribed Escitalopram (brand name Lexapro) an anti-depressant used to treat anxiety and major depressive disorder. My doctor said it would take up to 6 weeks before I would feel any improvement. This would be the first of many medications I would try over the next decade.

Medication compliance

I would find out the hard way that tinkering with my medication had catastrophic results. Medications form the foundation for building a comprehensive and effective maintenance treatment plan for individuals with bipolar disorder.

Looking back now I do wonder why I went on a self-sabotage mission. I have two dogs, a black Labrador called JD and a border collie called Scottie. Now and again, they get sick, and I have to bring them to the vet. The last occasion they had mites, so the vet prescribed medication to give to them. Not for one minute, did I think, to hell with it I'm throwing that medication away. I didn't question the vet's credentials by deciding that the dogs only needed half the medication. I meticulously followed the vet's instructions administrating the medication at the correct times twice a day.

Why did I follow the vet's instructions? I like my dogs. The last thing I wanted was to see them in pain. Yet I never took the medication as exactly prescribed by my doctor or psychiatrist. So, in one way I cared more about my dogs' health than my own. If a friend of mine had any health condition and told me they were coming off their medication without telling their clinician, I'd tell them that's a very poor choice.

So again, I asked myself how I had arrived at this ill-advised decision. I almost felt I could prove the medical practitioners wrong, that I could remain stable without the medication. My decision was born out of ignorance. Deep down I hated being on medication. No way was I going to take this chemical cocktail for the rest of my life. I was adamant that I didn't need it. I couldn't have been anymore wrong.

It would be a few years later that I would learn that anyone who has two or more episodes of bipolar disorder, generally is considered to have lifelong bipolar disorder. The focus shifts from not only treating current symptoms but also preventing future episodes. I would need drug therapy indefinitely.

From research I have looked at, coming off medication is a global phenomenon. It's not just unique to me. In the UK more than 60% of people with bipolarity come off their medication at some stage in their lives (Smith, 2018). Worldwide it's 70% I was fortunate I had very few side effects long-term. Initially I had some side effects as my body became used to the new medication. I experienced common side effect such as nausea, dry mouth, and an upset stomach. These stopped after six weeks. All I currently experience is a bit of drowsiness on awakening. Some people have horrible side effects, and you could see why they would be tempted to go cold turkey. The medication to control hypomania can lead to a lot of weight gain. Fortunately, I was never affected in this way.

Once I got myself well, I convinced myself that the medication had done its job. There was no need to keep taking the medication. I really should have heeded my psychiatrist's advice: "The medication that got you well keeps you well". My thinking was, if I do all the rights things such as eating well, abstaining from alcohol, regular exercise, and good sleep hygiene this would keep the illness at bay. If my diagnosis were mild depression, this strategy probably would have been enough. This wouldn't be the case for my bipolar illness.

2014 Paddy's weekend would be my first self-sabotage mission post diagnosis. It would take close to a week for the medication withdrawal symptoms to subside. The toughest element was that my sleep was completely disrupted. Even though I wasn't on sleeping pills the quetiapine I took to prevent the hypomanic episodes had a sedating effect which aided sleep. My sleep returned to normal after a week, so in my eyes the risk had paid off. I still felt well without taking the medication. I had single-handedly guaranteed myself a relapse. My psychiatrist told me previously that the brain cells didn't like someone altering their medication.

My illness was very subtle at times. It would take up to six months for me to come crashing down. In hindsight the warning signs were there. After a couple of weeks, I had become very irritable and snappy towards people around me, particularly with work colleagues.

I would still attend my psychiatrist's bi-monthly appointments. I would lie through my teeth about taking my medication. So, on the face of it everything was rosy. The cracks were slowly appearing. At the time it felt that suddenly out of nowhere, a train would hit me head on, leaving only remnants of my former self. I would attribute the relapse to a stressful job. I was missing the elephant in the room.

I saw the medication as a sign of weakness. None of my other mates needed a crutch and why should I? Some of the talk therapists I spoke to, had a very negative opinion of medication. They believed that medication dampened the emotions. This suited my narrative of being anti-medication and it was more evidence to rationalise coming off my meds. There was no reason for bipolarity. You were simply born with it, a chemical imbalance.

The way the illness works, after another relapse it would take longer to recover. I didn't realize on that Paddy's weekend I was playing with fire. When the wheels had fallen off, I informed my doctor and psychiatrist that I came off medication six months ago. It was too late. The damage was done. I was back to square one with crippling depression and suicidal thoughts every day for the next nine months. I had to go back on my medication. The process took time to get well again. I couldn't just return to the highest dose I was on previously. One of the main mood stabilisers I was on Lamotrigine had to start off on a very low dose which was increased slowly over six to eight weeks.

My actions had completely backfired. This would be a very harsh lesson. However, it would take one more lesson for me to finally take responsibility for my own condition. I would have to accept I'd be on medication for the rest of my life.

In October 2015 I would fully recover from my latest episode. I complied religiously with taking my medication for the next six months. Once again, this time around Easter I would start tinkering with my medication. I felt going cold turkey was too risky. I would halve the amount of medication I was taking. This would involve breaking up tablets, which was never a good idea. When I think back, it was ridiculous. The tablets were quite hard to break so I needed a strong knife to cut through them. Even if I had split them perfectly there was no saying that there was the same amount of medication in both halves. Everything was going according to plan, but like the last relapse there were early signs that things were going astray.

That August I went on holidays to Croatia. It was a

sweltering 37 degrees. I was having nightmares. I decided to come off the medication for that week. When I returned, I went back on a quarter of the medication I was prescribed. I felt I had taken a smart option, staying on a minimal amount of medication. Reducing my medication would over time have the exact impact as coming off them completely.

Once again, I relapsed in January 2017. This time I realized the magnitude of my poor decision. I returned to the clinic to let a psychiatric nurse know that, as she would say, I had been "slobbering" with my medication. I was in tears as I knew what was ahead of me. I didn't realize this time around it would take 20 months to recover fully from the relapse. This felt like the worst relapse of all. Talking to other people who had depressive episodes, we all agree that one of the hardest parts of the condition was just when you felt you had beaten the illness it came thundering back. Internally, I thought, I can't do this again. I had gone to the well too often.

The hardest part to accept was that I had brought this upon myself. This would be the last time I would ever come off or reduce my medication. I'm not sure how I managed to come through those 20 months alive. I have no doubt if in the future I alter my medication it will be fatal.

When I researched relapses after coming off medication unsupervised, I found that there is a 90%

chance of relapsing. I was an accident waiting to happen. Treatment for the illness is not an exact science but across the board, coming off medication on your own bat has dreadful consequences.

CHAPTER 4

The suspicious walking criminal

I was never that big into drinking but this one weekend in Galway I over indulged. A gang of us from college met up. It was a Saturday night in December 2016. The Christmas jumpers and the 12 pubs were in full flow. It was jammers everywhere. We settled for the Dail bar which had some standing space. I was a piss poor drinker. If I were caught in a big round, many a time I would wander off for a walk around the pub and drop a half pint on my way. That night I stuck to vodka and coke which I would regret.

We had booked into the Salthill hotel. We strolled back around 3am and headed to the resident's bar. There was a good atmosphere in the bar as the afters of a wedding were in full swing. I have no memories after that. The next thing I remember was one of the hotel staff knocking at the door after 11. Checkout was 11am so we had to get a move on. I made it to the toilet before throwing up.

Breakfast was well over as it was midday by the time

we checked out. I thought a bit of food might help so we hung around for the carvery lunch. I barely ate half of it, the turkey and ham didn't have the desired effect. The 100km drive home felt excruciatingly long.

I stopped off on the way home to throw up four times, what a mess. I stayed in my mate's house in Claremorris that night. I wasn't fit for much. Luckily, I had the Monday booked off from work. The Monday was a dark depressing December afternoon. I'd venture out for a walk.

I was walking down the road minding my own business. I was close to turning off on to the main road. Suddenly there's a jeep going slowly behind me.

What on earth does this clown want? I slowed down to snail pace and he slowed down accordingly. I crossed the road and he continued to follow me. He pulled up and rolled down the window

Are you alright?

I'm sound.

What are you at?

What do you think I'm at? I'm walking.

He barks back:

And where are you walking?

I don't know. I haven't made my mind up.

He slammed down on the accelerator and off he

went. It was like the Spanish inquisition. I kept walking. Twenty minutes later I was nearly home. A Garda's car passed me. I didn't take much notice. Next thing I could spot the cop's car doing a U-turn. He drove towards me. He pulled up beside me and hopped out. Once again:

What are you doing?

I wasn't in the form for this,

I'm out walking, is that a crime these days.

Well, we're after getting a report of a man matching your description out walking suspiciously. Such bullshit.

I don't know what you're talking about.

A female guard stepped out of the car to join the interrogation.

What's your name?

My name is Liam, guard.

Where are you living?

I'm not from here.

The guard wasn't going to let this go, she wouldn't be happy until I was in the back of the squad car. She roared at me again.

What's your second name?

Gildea is my second name.

She leapt into her car and put my name into their Pulse system. Not a thing popped up.

I've my eye on you Mr Gildea.

Good for you I thought.

They left it at that and told me to consider this a warning.

It could only happen to me. Of course, I thought I was completely innocent at the time. In fairness I did very little wrong. However, I didn't help my situation by speaking down to the guards. I also antagonised the guy who reported me. In my defence he had no right to interrogate me. In the bigger scheme of things this was a tell-tale sign that a bout of depression was on the way. When I got into arguments with people, the hypomania was transcending from a feeling of elation to a constant state of irritability. Looking back the illness always followed that pattern.

Why bother?

In periods of clinical depression my thoughts were, why bother with life? It is nothing but suffering and nobody gets out alive anyways. There's 7.7 billion people in the world. What did it matter if I drop dead? My career is in the toilet. After 10 years of doing exams, here I am queuing to pick up my dole on a Tuesday afternoon. This was it for me. A lifetime of not holding down a job and being a social pariah. Well into my 30s and living at home with my parents.

I felt like I was nothing but an embarrassment. Soon enough I wouldn't be able to afford to run a car. I would lose my independence all together. As for a relationship, two had ended in the last few years because of my illness. I had pulled the plug on both relationships. I just didn't see any good reason for being in one. What was the point of getting involved with someone again? As far as I was concerned, I was just wasting another person's time. It wasn't fair on them to be dating someone with a mental illness. I didn't intend to be alive for too much longer. I was doing them a favour; they wouldn't have to attend my funeral. They could move on with their lives.

Playing sport or going to the gym, why bother? I would drag myself into the gym, something when well, I enjoyed. There was never a voice of reason in my head challenging this pit of negativity about every hobby I once enjoyed. It was as if any positive rhetoric was outside of my vocabulary's reach. My energy would be zapped by the time I had changed my clothes. I'd walk into the gym with nobody else there. It was a weekday afternoon, there were no other losers who weren't working. I'd spend five minutes before leaving. I had no power in my body to lift anything.

I always loved going to Mayo matches but not when severely depressed. I recall my cousin bringing me to a Galway game in 2013. We hammered them. The game was over at half time. There was a huge crowd. My thoughts were why on earth would people be bothered going to a game? What enjoyment could they possibly get out of this? Funnily, if I were in a hypomanic episode this would have been a day to savour. Hammering the daylights out of our rivals. I even questioned the players as to why they bother, sure we never end up winning anything anyways.

One time I'd love sitting down to watch a good film. Now I would see it as one of the most futile things going. How would watching a film do anything to enhance my life? Friends would call me. I wouldn't answer the phone. Why bother having a conversation when I had nothing positive to say for myself? Anyway, they're probably only ringing me out of pity.

The outlook was extremely bleak. My mind couldn't

make one good argument for living on. My family would be better off without me sticking around. I was nothing but a hindrance. These severe existential crises were never ending. I felt I was rapidly going down a swallow hole.

Guilt and shame

For me, these emotions went hand and hand. However, they only came to the fore in the depressive episodes. I didn't have time in a hypomanic episode for reflection. I was in the prime of my life but had years where I thought the only relief would be to take my own life. I felt guilty that I had no appreciation of life. There were people out there fighting with other long-term illnesses and winning the battle. I had succumbed to my mental illness at a whimper.

I had become a drain on my family. In periods of long-term recovery, I had to live at home rent free. I had spent any savings I had, in my previous hypomanic episode. All my friends were getting on well with their lives. They had built up successful careers. Why did I have to get dealt such a bad hand in life?

When I became unemployed, I felt guilty that I was sponging off the state. I was ashamed by the fact I couldn't hold down a job. When I saw people with other disabilities working, I felt a complete failure. The voice in my head would tell me I was weak. How could I not be fit to work when other people far less fortunate, were well capable of holding a job?

With every episode that happened I felt an ever-increasing level of shame. My shame spoke a very convincing narrative. I was a poor excuse of a person.

Shame prevented me from self-compassion and acknowledgement of my illness. For years I didn't see my condition as an illness but a character flaw and weakness. In retrospect this made it harder to respond effectively to my illness and to realise that there were options available.

How, after gaining all the knowledge about bipolar illness from a professional mental health team, had I once again relapsed? I felt guilty that after all the effort from the nurses to get me well, that I just threw it away. I didn't believe I was worthy of people helping me to get well once again. The more severe my depression, the further I would ruminate on past events and poor decisions I took. This in turn would lead to further negative thinking and I would spiral into a more severe depression.

When my depression was at its worst, talk therapy was not an option. I didn't have the level of concentration needed to partake. I was left sitting with extremely intrusive thoughts of guilt and shame. When depressed hours felt like days. It felt like a never-ending hell. There was no chance of ever escaping.

Media portrayal

Recently in mass media, we've witnessed great leaps of awareness about relatively common mental-health issues such as depression and anxiety. With that awareness, there has been a decline in the negative attitudes that used to surround them. These are now readily discussed without shame. They are mostly represented in the media with a well-informed grasp of the facts, thanks to effective information campaigns.

However, severe mental health conditions, such as psychosis and bipolar illness remain shrouded in stigma and are consistently misrepresented and misunderstood.

The media tend to focus on the dramatic side of bipolar. In the early stages of my diagnosis, I felt embarrassed by the misrepresentation of the illness. The levels of behaviour depicted in manic periods, was not something I could relate to. For someone who has not experienced bipolar disorder it paints an inexact picture of what the sufferer is going through.

One of my favourite films recently was Joker. After the iconic performance of Heath Ledger as the joker in Batman Returns, I felt no actor could ever reach these heights. Joaquin Phoenix comes very close in this latest adaptation. He plays Arthur Fleck, a failed stand-up comedian whose descent into insanity and nihilism sparks a violent tirade. There is a strong mental health theme throughout the film. Unfortunately, Joker subscribes to the myth that serious mental illness and extreme violence go hand in hand.

In fact, people with severe mental illness are more vulnerable to violence *from* others than the general population. The film did get some things right such as nodding towards the lack of funding for mental health and the acute pain brought on by a severe mental illness. There's also a great quotation that resonates with me. "The worst part of having a mental illness is people expect you to behave as if you don't."

Joaquin rightly got an Oscar for best actor. It's just a shame that at times the mental health inaccuracies undermines his spellbinding performance.

Studies have found that over half of all mentally ill characters in TV and movies were portrayed as being dangerous to others. The American media are very keen to portray any individual involved in a mass shooting as having mental health issues. The reality according to the American Psychological Association is that shootings by people with serious mental health issues represent less than 1% of all gun related homicides each year.

There has been a small improvement in the last 5 years. Directors of TV shows now spend time to research bipolar illness. They involve people with mental health issues as part of their research. Whilst I've seen characters having full manic episodes, I have yet to see a character in a hypomanic state.

One Irish soap depicted a character having a manic episode. On one occasion he went out and bought nine TVs. Whilst I understand the logic, it portrays the character as unhinged. Excessive spending is a characteristic of bipolar. I believe it could have been portrayed more accurately if say buying an expensive car that a person couldn't afford, rather than buying nine of the same items. Then again soaps live off dramatic story lines.

I've seen ill-advised journalists writing for national newspapers referring to bipolar II as a made-up illness. I have to say this infuriates me that a journalist would write an article on a sensitive subject and do no research. It was a condition that celebrities clung on to, which helped them explain strange behaviour. Is it any wonder people think it's an illness of choice, if this is the drivel being written?

Sections of the media also make sweeping generalisations such as all people with schizophrenia hallucinate. Only between 60% and 80% of people with schizophrenia experience auditory hallucinations. An even smaller number of people experience visual hallucinations.

As with stigma we are moving in the right direction but we've a long way to go. I have done some media work in a bid to chip away at the lack of understanding of the illness. In particular, the older generations will forever associate mental illness with asylums. There is shame embedded in that section in society which will never be fully erased.

CHAPTER 5

Online dating

It was late 2009 when I became aware of online dating in the middle of a hypomanic period. In the following decade this would be the most glaringly obvious trait that my hypomania was spinning out of control. I was always able to rationalise it. I was a single man in my mid-twenties, why shouldn't I have a bit of fun? With every month that passed online dating was becoming increasingly popular, particularly in the bigger towns and cities My hypomanic episodes were like a hurricane, the episodes quickly built momentum.

I inadvertently stumbled across online dating, of all places, on the Irish times website. I had tired of chatting up random women on nights out in a night club, where you couldn't hear a thing anyone was saying. Straight away I liked this concept. There was no second guessing whether there was a boyfriend in play. At the time I was living in Mayo and going to college a lot of weekends in Dublin. I wasn't working, so I had a lot of time to explore dating websites. Most of the website members were based in Dublin which suited me. You could send one message to someone you came across. After that you had to pay a monthly fee for the service. That was the end of that. Surely there were free websites out there.

It wasn't long before I noticed Facebook had a form of online dating. It was here where I got my first online date. I was hooked. For the next five years in my hypomanic periods, online dating would take priority over everything else in my life.

Overtime I would see the link between bipolar and increased libido. I didn't realize how common this symptom was. Officially it's called hypersexuality and is listed as one of the diagnostic criteria for bipolar disorder. Online dating interfered with other parts of my life. I would be sending messages at 3am in the morning with work the following day. During work hours I would be doing the same. It's very common for people with bipolar disorder to wreak havoc in their relationships. People who would always have been faithful, now are cheating on their partners. Thankfully, I was single for these years. When I did have a girlfriend, it tended to coincide with a depressive episode so the likelihood of me cheating was zero. My libido would disappear in a matter of weeks.

I had difficulty in controlling my sexual urges in hypomanic periods. I was a very confident person in these short-lived periods. I didn't waste any time in going on online dates. I was too impatient to wait longer than a week. Like everything else, I wanted instant gratification. I wouldn't consider that it was a sexual addiction. I only experienced hypersexuality as often as I experienced hypomania which induced it. With sexual addiction, there isn't any lull. A person must live with the condition daily.

As I had been single, on the face of it I was doing nothing out of the ordinary. At the time I never questioned my behaviour. Obviously, it wasn't normal behaviour driving two hours for a date in Sligo on a Tuesday evening. I got caught up in the whole thing. The number of dates increased in line with the more elated I became. A few of the lads knew I was online dating but didn't know the actual extent to which it was consuming me. At the height of it I was having three dates per week ranging anywhere from Mayo during the week to Drumcondra in Dublin on a Saturday night. Any girlfriend I've had has been through online dating. It has its positives. It was my place of mind rather than the dating sites themselves that was the issue.

As with nearly every other symptom on the bipolar spectrum, when depressed the complete opposite was the case. I didn't see the point of online dating; it was the last thing on my mind. The idea of striking a conversation with a random stranger was nauseating. Even the thought of it would bring on a wave of anxiety. When depressed I felt ugly. I had no confidence in interacting with my best friends or partner, never mind random strangers.

I would be the first to admit that it is very difficult to be in a relationship with a person who has bipolar illness if the condition isn't under control. As time passed my low mood began to cause issues in my relationships. It was hard for my partner to understand how my libido had disappeared. Of course, they thought I had lost interest in them. This wasn't the case, as with everything else in my life I had no interest in anything.

Rachel: America's First Lady

January 2012, as was par for the course, I had entered another hypomanic episode. I was living outside Galway city in Roscam with a few hurlers from Galway. There was five of us, all single, so it was a lively house to say the least. They were very opinionated but there was great banter.

I had recommenced my online dating escapades. I had taken a break since June 2011. I had had a severe bout of depression for the remainder of that year. It really set me back. Every depressive relapse felt worse than the previous one. I tried my best to forget that the previous depressive episodes ever happened. I had to pull out of my final accounting exams coupled with the unfortunate loss of a job due to a company closure. I was forced to move home. When the external factors were piled upon the clinical depression, it emotionally floored me. Christ, they were a horrible few months.

But back to 2012, I was in full flow, there were numerous dates. At this stage I had moved on to the Plenty of Fish online platform. POF, as it was widely known, had taken over the online dating scene. It had no main competitors until Tinder arrived in September later than year. All the cool kids were now online dating. It was no longer seen as in anyway taboo. By the time February came, I was back to having a few dates every week, although this time I mostly dated in Galway.

Rachel from Washington was worth noting, a very attractive lady. I always used a sincere approach, a lot of other lads, from what I heard, were very crass to say the least. Girls tended to converse with me in a normal way. No woman would have picked up from our early interactions that there was anything untoward about me. It came across as my personality type. I had a lot to get off my chest when dating, so rapid speech was the norm.

I sent a long introductory message to Rachel. She replied immediately, which was always a good sign. First off, she told me she was from Washington and was currently living there. She worked in the White House under Obama's administration. She seemed a very interesting lady. To my delight she was moving to Galway in the coming weeks.

I soon learned that this lady certainly wasn't shy. We were getting on well. She asked me for my email address so we could exchange current pictures. It is human nature to send pictures of ourselves looking better than we do. I always felt unattractive. Even in my current exuberant mode, poor body image for the last 15 years had taken its toll on my confidence.

Anyhow we exchanged pictures. I was in for a big

surprise. My interpretation was 'Here's a photo of me outside Old Trafford in 2007 looking happy'. Rachel's interpretation was 'Here's a photo of me with no clothes on'.

Rachel was coming home in two weeks' time and I was to meet her in Dublin. She was going to do some travelling before she moved to Galway. She had checked into a top hotel in Dublin for the week, money didn't seem to be an issue.

Then there was an unusual twist. She sent me an apologetic email. She had met someone else on a night on the town and that was it. She was smitten by some guy from Carlow. She seemed desperate to settle down with any Irish fella that showed any interest in her. Oh well, I wished her the best of luck, no hard feelings. It wasn't uncommon for people to pull out of dates on POF at the last second.

I thought that was the end of Rachel. She had told me she had got engaged the following month and was to be married on the May bank holiday in 2012 without her dad's approval. His opinion was that the marriage would be gone by Christmas. He was funding the whole thing. There is a big tradition in America that the father's bride pays for the wedding. That tradition never made it across the Atlantic to Irish brides. I did think it was a bit rushed. She had only known him for three months, but she seemed to know what she wanted.

I sent an email to Rachel wishing her all the best in married life the week before the wedding. I was out for a run in Galway down by the prom a few months later. My phone started vibrating in my pocket. I pulled in for a coffee. It was Rachel. The marriage was already on the rocks. Ironically, her new hubby had got depressed since they got married. He showed no interest in Rachel physically and otherwise. My heart went out to her, it was a tough break.

I advised Rachel to stick by her man, he'll come out of his depression over time. As a couple you'll be stronger for it, I told her. She wasn't having it. Citing his zero interest in her physically, she brought the relationship to breaking point.

My birthday was coming up in mid-August. She was aware of that, as we were friends on Facebook. She started emailing me, cumulating in a video camera propped on a shelf looking directly down on her whilst she soaked in a bubble bath. How she was going to explain that if her hubby walked in, I don't know.

Then came the proposal. Without telling me, she had booked the Sheraton hotel in Athlone as a birthday present on the Saturday of my birthday. She wanted to hook up. I was no angel but sleeping with a married woman even in the middle of a hypomanic episode was a step too far. I fought against my promiscuous ways. For once I made the right decision. Over the next few weeks, she gradually stopped contacting me. I had made it very clear to her at that stage that us sleeping together wasn't going to happen.

I sent her an email six months later. She had moved back to Washington with hubby and things were fantastic once again. There's a way of thinking in society now, unlike the previous generation, people seem unwilling to work through a tough period in their relationship. If we had hooked up, the marriage was gone. I haven't heard from Rachel since. If I had to bet whether that marriage would last I'd be inclined to say no.

On reflection it was a strange incident which really summed me up when I was hypomanic. I tended to be right bang in the middle of some woman's drama.

Anger

Anger is a very unpleasant characteristic of the hypomanic side of the illness. I used to switch from being irritable to being a very angry individual at the drop of a hat. I would argue with anyone that would slightly cross me. I'd be adamant that I was right on every occasion. I would have countless arguments in the space of a week.

Once this stage kicked in, the real enjoyable highs were a distant memory. I caused a lot more havoc in these periods, than I ever did in my most severe periods of depression. When depressed I was withdrawn and would have little interaction with people.

In November 2008 my behaviour caused a lot of trouble at work. Thankfully, I never physically attacked someone but looking back there were underlying signs of passive aggression. In one job I was working with five people in an open office plan. In general, we had good working relationships. I had been depressed a lot in that job. Family members generally say it is far easier to deal with their loved one, when they are depressed as opposed to being hypomanic

One by one, I had arguments with my work colleagues usually over petty stuff. Of course, they didn't fully understand what was going on. I'd imagine they just put it down to me being an asshole.

I spoke down to them which wasn't well received and why should it be? Now it takes two to tango, but I was always the instigator. Eventually it got to the stage where I had totally alienated myself in the office.

I felt at the time they had ganged up on me. Eventually one of the partners called me in and asked me to apologize to one of my work colleagues. I did apologize, but the damage was done. As it happened two months later, I would be let go from that job. My contract expired and the recession had hit the country with venom. There wasn't any work but even if there was, I had become a big problem. I had to be shown the door. Someone roaring and shouting has no place in any workplace.

I also became cranky when dealing with customers. This was unacceptable. HR in one company did raise their concerns on this matter and gave me a verbal warning. I felt at the time it was the customer who was difficult and lied. As was always the case, I felt I did nothing wrong.

Dealing with people in a consumer situation was another area in my life where I could wreak havoc. I was very reactive and demanding of other people. As mentioned before in December 2008 I ran up a phone bill of €527. I went through any employee I dealt with. I was completely ignorant and incredibly difficult to deal with.

My first port of call was to attack a manager. I refused to take any responsibility for my actions. Eventually he hung up on me. No way was I going to let this go. I went to the nearest phone shop in the middle of the working day telling my boss I had an emergency. I was so aggressive towards the customer assistant that the manager intervened. I continued to rant at him without avail. I stormed out nearly taking the hinges off the door with me. It was disgraceful behaviour. I really let myself down. At the time it felt perfectly normal.

Another incident that occurred at the same time was the purchase of a very expensive jacket. On Christmas day whilst leaning against the fireplace, I was unaware that there was a candle directly behind me. You guessed it, my brand-new jacket went up in flames. I had to wait until after Stephen's day to go back to the shop where I purchased the jacket. I carried the tatters of a jacket in with me. I immediately went down the customer's assistant's throat. I'm sure I frightened him, as that day in particular, I was extremely aggressive. I mentioned that a jacket of a €100 shouldn't have gone up in flames as easily. Anyway, I wanted the identical jacket. To my dismay they had none left.

I demanded that he call one of the stores in Dublin to check for availability. He refused and asked why I was being so aggressive. Once again, I demanded that he make the phone call so they could courier the jacket down the following day. At this stage he was becoming visibly upset and yet again a manager had to intervene.

The manager coaxed me into looking at different jackets. Eventually I bought one. I thanked her for her help. I told her that her staff member wasn't fit for the job. It was bizarre behaviour. I was a bad mix of grandiosity and arrogance and a nightmare to deal with. At the time I felt the whole world was conspiring against me. I wasn't going to let people walk all over me. Unsurprisingly, an episode of depression was imminent. When it hit six weeks later, I reflected on my behaviour with utter shame and embarrassment.

My impending depression was hidden under a mask of anger. I've heard people say that depression and anger are two sides of the same coin. Anger is depression with enthusiasm and depression is anger without enthusiasm. Particularly in men, it seems that many of us express emotional issues in a wrath of anger.

CBT

One of the most successful talk therapies for bipolar illness is Cognitive Behavioural Therapy. It's more commonly referred to as CBT. It focuses on the way people think and act to help them overcome their emotional and behavioural problems (Beck, 2011). It teaches you to observe the way your behaviour and thoughts can affect your mood. It helps you identify automatic negative thoughts. It then works to build new habits that help you to feel better. CBT's reputation as a highly effective treatment for all mental health issues is growing. CBT for bipolar disorder typically consists of 12 to 20 individual sessions over a period of 6 months

A central concept in CBT is that you feel the way you think. Therefore, CBT works on the principle that you can live more happily and productively if you're thinking in healthy ways.

- Cognitive means mental processes like thinking. The word 'cognitive' refers to everything that goes on in your mind including dreams, memories, images, thoughts, and attention.
- Behaviour refers to everything that you do. This includes what you say, how you try to solve problems, how you act, and avoidance.

- Therapy is a word used to describe a systematic approach to combating a problem, illness, or irregular condition.

CBT teaches a person how to challenge these negative thoughts. Are you being more critical of yourself than another person would be? The only thing with bipolar and most other mental health conditions is you must be well to participate in the sessions. If you are very depressed, your concentration won't be good enough to process the information you're receiving. More importantly, putting this into practice in your daily life requires that you be stable.

On a couple of occasions, I had a CBT or a psychology appointment coming up only for my nurse to intervene and postpone the appointment. I was so depressed that I struggled to read the paper. Two years ago, I did six sessions. I worked on assertiveness. This also tied into self-confidence. I do not like conflict. I'm too agreeable. I've since learned how to stand up for myself in situations where I feel people are taking advantage. I am always trying to please others which isn't always an advantage if it's to the detriment of myself. I've realised I have to speak my own truth whether this is to the liking of other people or not. I don't assume my initial thoughts are always based on facts. A lot of my life I have lived in the hypothetical world, now I'll only engage with actual facts.

I've also became aware of a cognitive distortion that has been with me for many years called a mental filter. It is a term used to describe one type of cognitive distortion, or faulty thought pattern. This can often lead to higher levels of anxiety and depression. When thinking through a mental filter, a person is focusing only on the negative aspects of a situation and filtering out all of the positive ones (Star, 2019). Following a job interview, I will only recall criticism and not all the positive feedback. I now veer away from this black or white thinking and try to be more objective.

There is ample material online in relation to CBT. I find I can go through this by myself and practise the methods suggested such as working on my value system. However, I do believe face to face therapy is more effective, particularly for the first few sessions. It is particularly effective for any anxiety disorders. Thankfully, since I've been well, I have had no issues with anxiety. Different therapists have different approaches. I know one lady who has bad anxiety and was seeing a therapist. She had different tasks to complete in between sessions. One was to walk into a coffee shop and ask a stranger if she could join them for a coffee. Her take was 'What normal person does that?' Another task was to queue up in Tesco and if there were a few people behind her, to ask the cashier to explain the club points system. The therapist focused in on what she was feeling and the thoughts that were going through her head. Whilst his methods were a little unusual, I can understand the logic of it. Both were anxiety provoking situations. The real work was just beginning.

I think CBT is very helpful particularly in the early stage of most mental illnesses. I've no doubt I would have got a better handle on my condition had I been aware of CBT 10 years ago.

Unlike other therapies the patient must do homework between the sessions, for it to be effective. CBT is solely focused on your current issues. At no stage is it meant to reflect on things such as what happened in your childhood.

Dialectical Behaviour Therapy (DBT) has proven useful in teaching patients how to regulate their emotions. DBT is based on CBT but with more focus on regulating emotions, being mindful and learning to accept pain.

CHAPTER 6

A cocktail of medication

When I was close to suicide, I was usually on a cocktail of five different medications. 2013 would be the first time that I wasn't solely being treated with anti depressants. As I hadn't been sleeping, straight away I was put on sleeping pills to help me nod off. I woke up very groggy. I felt like I had a hangover. Still, it was better than no sleep. It knocked me out for a few hours. I got a break from the suicidal thoughts.

For the short term I would be put on an anti-depressant to begin the process of recovery. I was put on 20mgs of Prozac. In the coming weeks I would gradually go up to the highest dose of 40mgs. This would eventually kick start my mood. All psychiatrists tend to have their favourite anti-depressant drug. Prozac came out in 1987. It was one of the first of a new type of anti-depressant (SSRI). There was no end of choice when it came to picking an anti-depressant. There had to be careful monitoring of the dose of Prozac I was taking. This medication would only be a short-term measure. In 2013, five months would prove long enough for the medication to lift me out of severe depression. For anyone with a bipolar illness, long term use of a strong anti-depressant can cause a medicated high. This was the case in this incident. My mood rocketed, so I was taken off Prozac very quickly in August of that year.

At my most depressed, I also became extremely anxious. My anxiety would be treated with clonazepam. This medication is also used to prevent and control seizures. Clonazepam works by calming your brain and nerves. It increases levels of a calming chemical (GABA) in your brain. This is a benzodiazepine medication, commonly referred to on the streets as Benzos. I would take this twice a day to ease my anxiety. It was a nice feeling after taking this medication. Unlike anti-depressant medication, I could feel the effect within an hour. My anxiety dropped for a few hours. The only issue with clonazepam was that it was an addictive medication. It was used as a short-term relief.

Long term, there were a few choices as to what medication could be taken. The staple medication for bipolar illness since the early 1950's has been lithium. Australian psychiatrist, John Cade, first suggested in 1949 that lithium could be used to treat depressive type episodes. He also demonstrated that it could calm manic symptoms (Levine, 2012). Doctors don't know exactly how lithium works to stabilize a person's mood. It is thought to help strengthen nerve cell connections in brain regions that are involved in regulating mood, thinking and behaviour.

Lithium is a salt that leaves the body through the kidneys, unlike most medications which go through the liver. The main issue with lithium is its toxicity. Not everyone can tolerate it because either it's not right for one's body or another condition precludes them from taking it. Even if the drug is right for a person, it's unusual in that the amount necessary to be effective is only slightly less than the amount that makes it toxic.

Lithium has both a preventive and treatment effect. Research suggests that a distinguishing feature of lithium is that it has the strongest data of any mood stabilizer for the reduction of suicide. For 80-90% of people, lithium will prevent a manic episode (McKeon, 2018). If you start taking lithium and then stop abruptly, the scientific evidence suggests you will have more episodes of mania than you would have had if you never took it at all (Craddock, 2012).

Up until then I had never been treated with lithium. I would be treated with two different medications that would help stabilize my mood long term. The first was Quetiapine which was an atypical antipsychotic also used to treat schizophrenia. It is a relatively new medication that came on to the market in 1997. This acts as a mood stabiliser which primarily prevents episodes of hypomania. There is also an anti-depressant base. Quetiapine is believed to work by rebalancing the brain chemicals dopamine and serotonin, to improve thinking, mood and behaviour. For me, it had the bonus of putting me to sleep quickly. The first night I took it, I was asleep by the time I reached the top of the stairs.

The other medication I take in conjunction with Quetiapine is Lamotrigine. This also was relatively new. It was approved for use in 2003. It was initially used for people who had seizures. It soon became apparent from testing, that it was effective for preventing the recurrent depressive episodes of bipolar illness.

Lamotrigine has a side effect of a severe and dangerous rash, so it would have to be introduced at a very low level until we hit the therapeutic dose. Progress was extremely slow. Long-term, taking both medications would prove very effective in the treatment of my illness. Once I came to terms with accepting that, I would be on both medications for the rest of my life.

The Roscommon Heist

I take you back to February 2014. I had weaned myself off my medication a few weeks earlier over the space of a week. I had only been stable for a mere three months. It was glaringly obvious that the medication brought on the stability. At the time I refused to acknowledge the science. This would be my first time coming off mood stabilisers as opposed to anti-depressants in previous years. I was still struggling to understand the devastating effect of coming off medication and allowing a hypomanic episode to go untreated.

Over the coming years there would be serious consequences for my ill-informed choices. Being hypomanic was a fantastic feeling. I had buckets of energy, a swagger and a confidence that I only could have dreamt of in a depressive episode. It was such a relief to see the back of the last depressive chapter.

Anyhow, back to this plenty of fish encounter. I was working locally so was living at home. My manic side was showing signs of gradually reappearing. A far subtler version of me but just as dangerous, if not more so. The illness had learnt to be more conniving. I believe I was in denial, that deep down I couldn't accept the fact that I had a long-term mental illness. I put the severe depressive episode in 2013 down to being just a difficult stage of life I got through.

So, I started messaging this lady living locally who had caught my eye. She was about two years younger than me and said she went to my school, but I had never seen her before. I was a bit suspicious as I'd know a good-looking girl in a small town where I had lived and grown up. I forwarded her photo on to a few school mates but none of them knew her to see. It made me extremely wary of her. Something just seemed a tad off with her. The conversation didn't seem to follow a typical flow. She said she had just joined Plenty of Fish at Christmas as she was newly single. She said she wasn't looking to get into a serious relationship, which I had no issue with. I had to give her the benefit of the doubt and take her at her word.

We organised a date on a Monday evening in Ballinlough, the village next to us. Monday is always a depressing day in the office, especially when you worked in accounts and it is month end. It gave me something to look forward to. Then a few messages that morning. She wanted to go for lunch instead. That wasn't an option for me. We kept with the original plan.

We were going to meet up outside the Whitehouse Hotel, which was no longer open, at 7pm. We'd decide our course of action for the evening then. At 5pm that evening came a late request for an explicit photo. I declined. This just made me more suspicious of what this girl's story was. I got home from work at 6pm and got ready quickly. Oddly, we hadn't exchanged numbers at this stage, so it was strictly POF messages. At 7pm, I pulled up outside the hotel, I had the POF app on my phone, so I sent her a quick message to say I had arrived. Still no sign of her. I said I'd give her another five minutes to reply to me before I headed home. My phone vibrated. She said she was walking towards me and she'd be there in a minute. I still didn't see her. Then she said she was further down the street. This set alarm bells off. I messaged, "Look if I don't see you in the next 30 seconds forget about it."

Another change of plan; she was now in her house and her parents had gone out. She was really pulling the piss at this stage. She told me the location of the house and the yellow door which were accurate. She said to knock on the door, and she'd meet me there. I told her to come to the door and when I saw her, I'd go to the house. She was full of crap. Then another message: "There's a side road just down by my house I'm waiting down there for you in my car. We can have some fun."

There was a side road but who the hell was at the bottom of the road? Was this some idiot from school setting me up for a fall? I told her to get lost and I drove home. It bugged me for days after, who the hell was she. Was there a group of lads trying to ridicule me? It couldn't be, too much effort went into it. Was she even from the area? Then how was she able to give me exact directions to that house? Whose house was that and were they in on the prank?

A few weeks later a story was going viral, and the puzzle was solved. A gang from the midlands was setting up fake profiles on Plenty of Fish of stunning looking girls. They lured fellas just like me into an attempted heist. A lot of guys got done, the wallet, watch and even the car in a few cases. I now knew who was waiting for me at the end of that road. It all made sense.

I should have gone with my gut and not gone on the date in the first place. When I was beginning to enter the hypomanic phase of the illness, my decision making left a lot to be desired. All I saw was the instant gratification. That clouded my judgement on so many occasions. At least I wasn't stupid enough to drive down that small road. Christ, I was lucky! Imagine the embarrassment if I had to call home, that I had got jumped by a gang and the car gone.

Celebrities and Bipolar

Mental illness isn't choosy; it affects every facet of society. One of my favourite English actors and writers is Stephen Fry. He has a bipolar diagnosis. He does great work on raising awareness of bipolarity. He has done several documentaries which are a fascinating insight.

He compares his depressive symptoms to the weather. Depression is like the rain, it's nothing you've done or decided to do. You can't wish it away. It's raining, my life is over. You cannot imagine a future.

When depressed he just wants to be on his own and doesn't want to interact with anyone. He takes lithium every day. For the most part it works very well. Now and again, he tips over into mania. He describes his mania as a type of grandiosity, energy, and hyperactivity. There's an optimism, the exact opposite to a period of depression.

He has quoted the poet J. W. Jordan:

"Don't take my devil away because my angels may flee too."

In his documentary he spoke to 43 different people in the acting world with the disorder. He offered them the hypothetical choice to press a button to get rid of their illness. Only one person would press the button.

In 2015 he interviewed Carrie Fisher who has since died. She spoke very candidly about her battle with bipolar illness.

Bipolar Disorder can be a great teacher. It's a challenge, but it can set you up to be able to do almost anything else in your life. Scientists are now saying that growing evidence suggest that people who are genetically predisposed to bipolar disorder are more likely than others to show high levels of creativity, in particularly in artistic fields where strong verbal skills are helpful (Reid, 2012).

When it comes to creativity in most senses, I don't have that special intelligence required. I do see creativity in some places in my life. I think I can write to a satisfactory level and can think outside the box to improve things in my work life. I know people with bipolar that are the most fantastic artists. Breath taking work, I couldn't do it justice to explain the pictures they paint.

In one study from 2015, researchers took the IQ of almost 2,000 eight-year-old children. They then assessed them at ages 22 or 23 for manic traits. They found that high childhood IQ was linked with bipolar symptoms later in life. For this reason, researchers believe the genetic features associated with bipolar disorder can be helpful in the sense that they also may produce beneficial traits. In another study in 2015, Trusted Source researchers analysed the DNA of more than 86,000 people to look for genes that increase the risks of bipolar disorder and schizophrenia. They found that creative individuals are up to 25 percent more likely than non-creative people to carry genes that are associated with bipolar and schizophrenia.

Examples of well-known people who were bipolar include:

- Winston Churchill- British prime minster 1940 - 1945 World War 2
- Vincent Van Gogh - Dutch painter
- Kurt Cobain - Ex Nirvana lead singer
- Russell Brand - English comedian

Celebrities run into trouble where they come off medication to access another hypomanic or manic episode. They believe they can access their more creative side when off medication.

CHAPTER 7

Stigma

There is great work being done on the ground level by mental health organisations. However mental illness stigma is still very ingrained in Irish society. Will there come a time when the stigma is fully erased? I think, like racism, it will always be present at some level.

There are more people sharing their mental health struggles publicly which is of great benefit. There are still a lot of Irish people who don't want to have that difficult conversation. People are comfortable with reading a story about someone who was depressed for a few months, stopped drinking, turned to running and have never been ill since. A lot of people have mental health difficulties every day of their adult lives. For many this is too close to the bone.

Stigma is particularly embedded in the older generations. Forty years ago, people didn't discuss their mental health issues with anyone. The sufferer was hidden away and not spoken about. He was treated as a social pariah. I'm not sure how the stigma originated. Did people think it was a mortal sin to feel life wasn't worth living? If it isn't bad enough to have a mental illness, for society then to make you feel ashamed is beyond cruel.

If you were in hospital recovering from a heart attack, all your friends and family would be in to visit bringing chocolate and good wishes. Compare this to someone who is in a mental health hospital recovering from a severe episode of mania. In the main, most people are uncomfortable visiting. I've seen first-hand parents not visiting their child out of shame and embarrassment. I asked them why they felt this way. They said they were afraid someone might see them coming out of the mental health facility.

In September 2017 Saint Patrick's Mental Health Services carried out a survey to analyse the extent of the mental health stigma in Ireland (Gilligan, 2017).

- Two thirds of respondents said being treated for a mental health issue was a sign of personal failure.
- Four in 10 of those surveyed wanted the public to be better protected from people with mental health problems.
- 44 per cent would not trust someone who experienced post-natal depression to babysit.
- A quarter would tell no one if they had previously been an inpatient for a mental health difficulty.

Even though 28% of the people surveyed had been treated for a mental health difficulty themselves, there was a predominantly negative attitude towards mental illness. Even more disconcerting was the fact that in 2006 when the same survey was carried out similar levels of stigma were found. Even though awareness of mental health difficulties has increased twofold, 11 years later, people with mental health issues are no less stigmatised.

Despite a steady stream of public information campaigns, a key question remains unanswered. What is it that prevents us from viewing psychological problems as we would any other health issue? How do we even try to turn things around? Whilst one can claim that people have a lack of knowledge of the illness, there is no denying we live in an era where information is freely available in a matter of seconds. People are choosing not to educate themselves. The adage 'ignorance is bliss' pops into my mind. It's easier to choose not to know the whole truth about the illness, thus absolving you from any blame for hurtful comments.

Education from an early age is key. Slowly, the school curriculum in Ireland is promoting mental health awareness amongst teenagers. Personally, I feel the work needs to be done from the age of five. You'd be surprised how quickly children can pick up any subject and understand it. The early years is the best time to instil a basic understanding of mental health, it will stick with them for the rest of their lives.

The Jesuits have a saying, 'give me the child for the first seven years and I'll show you the man'. I know a teacher and she does mindfulness with her class. She puts huge effort into focusing on self-esteem. She has a mental health corner in the classroom, and the kids love it. Between birth and the age of seven, our minds are like a sponge (Lipton, 2018). Whatever the behaviour is around us, we'll copy it. I believe it's easier to build a strong child than fix a broken adult.

One would hope that in 50 years' time people will wonder how ignorant we were as a society, where you were condemned for having an illness that was outside your control.

Low Self-Confidence and Sensitivity

Looking back, I always had issues with low self-confidence. I never felt good enough. I always felt inferior to other people. Where did it originate? Was it something I picked up in childhood? I genuinely don't know. It was never more present than in the periods of severe depression. That voice inside echoed all day long: "You deserve nothing, you piece of dirt."

Even in periods of being grandiose to the extreme, that voice was still there. It wasn't chattering as loudly, more so in the distance. There was always an undercurrent. I always felt I had to prove myself. Nothing I ever achieved would suffice. Now I ask the question "Who was I trying to impress?". It was an extremely tiring trait. I felt I was judged day in day out. The irony was that the only judge was me.

Counsellors would tell me that I didn't need anyone else's stick to beat myself with. I was an expert at that myself. I never took compliments well. I don't think Irish people do in general. It was an uncomfortable feeling. My first thought was, it must be sarcasm. If in the space of an hour, a friend was to compliment me and criticise me, the compliment wouldn't register in my mind. However, the criticism would last with me for years. To this day I can recall the criticism as if it was yesterday. In the Hindu tradition these are called a karmic experience. A karmic experience is anything that happens which generates a negative emotion. In this case, the criticism triggers the memory of that person saying those words and the unworthy feeling that goes with them. I guess I have my good memory to blame for storing those negative emotions.

It was a snowball effect, as the years passed by, the criticism sounded louder. In my mind every little bit of criticism that accumulated was stronger evidence that I was a piece of dirt.

I was always a sensitive child. It would take very little to make me cry. This was something that would always stay with me. I felt things harder than most other people. It was built into me. Whether this was an early sign of a mental illness or just how my childhood played out I'm not certain. Either way the result was the same, a human being who was extremely sensitive to criticism.

Along with being sensitive I was also a very anxious child. I was always worried about something. Even at the age of six or seven, I'd be worried about the next maths or spelling test. If we were having a school tour, I'd be anxious about where I would sit on the bus. The simplest of things caused me worry. Of course, at that age you're not aware of what's going on, it's just normal. Once one worry was over, another worry crept in. Whilst most children were out enjoying playing football, I'd be playing but my mind would be wandering to my next worry.

They say you become an expert at what you practise. The mind can't differentiate between a positive or negative practice. I practised hating myself and being anxious all day long. From an early age I had become an expert in all these aspects. I was laying the seeds for a person who I'd grow to despise.

The Chase

In May 2011 I was living in Galway and my mood had rocketed. I had one more month before things veered towards a vicious depression. My buddy Walt and I were out in Galway on a Saturday night. I was in college the next day in Dublin so I wouldn't be staying out too late. I was to keep my nose out of trouble.

Galway was jammers; we were down in An Púcán, a trendy bar just off the main street in Galway. There was barely breathing space inside, so we headed out to the smoking area. I never smoked in my life, but this was the place if you had intentions of meeting a woman in Galway on a Saturday night. We got chatting to two women, harmless enough stuff. I wasn't getting too involved as I knew I wasn't out for the night. Around 1am I left Walt to it and headed for home. I wasn't drinking so I had my car parked up off Eyre Square. The city was buzzing. The huge crowds in the pubs had spilled out to the streets.

I walked down by Supermac's. I had thoughts of going in for a feed, but the huge queues put me off. I spotted a stunner sitting on the footpath with a few of her friends. They all had their high heels thrown to the side. Fashion comes at a price. Pain. Brazenly I sat beside them as if I knew them for years. Boundaries never concerned me when I was elated. I was chatting away to her for 15 minutes and it was going nowhere fast, but I persisted.

I thought this woman had a bit of an attitude and told me to get lost. I didn't take too kindly to being spoken to like that particularly in the phase of the illness she caught me in. I told her to come down off her high horse, that it wasn't the catwalk in Milan she had walked off. That was the end of our interaction. I think she knew at that stage I was very hostile, so she didn't bite back. As I walked away, I heard two lads roaring at me. These were two of her fella mates who were hammered and weren't going to let my behaviour slide. They kept shouting obscenities at me. Eventually, I had had enough and turned around and gave them the finger. Another ill-advised decision which turned a nothing situation into something more dangerous.

I kept walking and the shouting had stopped or so it seemed. I turned around once more and saw the two boys running after me like Usain Bolt. Bollocks... I started to run. I had a good start on them, but they were a lot quicker than me. I was still a good distance away from the car. They were getting closer. The car was parked at the back of a small car park. We both hit the car park at the same side. I had 20 yards on them, I would just make the car in time. The problem was I was boxed in. I had to drive past them to get out.

Anxiety came over me. I knew I was in for a good beating and there wasn't another soul around to step in. I locked the car before I turned on the ignition. One of them tried to pull me out of the car. When he had no joy, he battered the windows with his fist. I had just got the car into gear before he attempted to jump up on the bonnet. I put the foot down. I didn't care if I took him with me. He jumped out of the way. The other knob had found a brick, I sped off with him chasing me. He bashed the brick into the side of my car causing a good bit of damage. Phew! I got away.

I was a little unlucky to have come across two thugs like that, but as always, I brought the situation upon myself. I was lucky that I wasn't beaten to death.

I drove to Dublin the following morning at 6am with just over four hours sleep. I was to attend an accounting lecture at 9.00am. I only realized how bad the damage to the car was that morning. I arrived in Dublin only to find out it was the following Sunday the lecture was on. That sums up a lot of what it's like to be hypomanic. My decision making was consistently poor, as it was in this case. I was a disorganized mess. I didn't even bother to look at the college timetable. I had looked at it earlier in the week, but my concentration was so poor, I had mixed up the dates.

CHAPTER 8

Unemployment

Most people practise some form of a daily routine. We don't tend to react well when that routine disappears. Herein lies the biggest issue when faced with unemployment. The first time I lost a job was in 2009. It was the beginning of the biggest recession to hit the country in a century. The arse had fallen out of the country. There were a thousand jobs being lost every week. My accounting training contract was finishing up at the time. There was no more work, so I had to be let go. At the time I was on a high, so it didn't really faze me. Over the coming years, the unemployment rate would grow to 15%.

I had accounting exams coming up in six months so I would focus on them while I had no work. I enjoyed the first few weeks off. I looked at it as a few weeks' holidays, not doing an awful lot. Unknown to me, my mood was deteriorating at an alarming rate. I finished up at the end of February. By the May bank holiday weekend, once again I was amidst a crippling depression.

For any person with or without a mental illness, unemployment can shake you to the core. A job is a form of identity. It's one of the first questions people ask when they meet you for the first time. Where do you work yourself? If you haven't met a friend for a while, how's work going?

I grew to hate being asked these questions. They ended up being a conversation killer. When you said you weren't working, the other person felt awkward for broaching the subject. For many people unemployment can bring on a period of depression. They may never have had any mental health issues before this. For someone like myself with severe depression, it just added to the torment.

A job is a lot more than earning an income. It gives people a sense of purpose and belonging. There's a reason to get yourself out of bed in the morning. You get to meet and engage with other people. There is a feeling of well-being that comes with work. You are part of a group that is contributing towards society. However, all this goes when you become unemployed. At the time my whole value system was centred on my career. It was the only yardstick I measured myself by.

This would be the first of many periods of unemployment. I blamed not having a job for my depression. If I had a job, I would be full of confidence and feel good within myself I told myself fifty times a day. I had replaced my skin issues with unemployment as the rational reason for my severe depression. Of course, unemployment was a challenging issue, but not the reason I felt I'd be better off dead.

According to statistics in Ireland between 30%-40% of people with bipolar disorder are unemployed (Murtagh, 2020). Of course, I always came across these statistics when I was low. This statistic reinforced my belief that I was a victim, and that my life was ruined.

Any sufferers of depression will tell you that mornings are exceptionally tough. If you don't have a reason to get up in the morning, there's more of a chance you'll stay in bed. The fact I had lost all interest in everything made the days excruciating long. When my depression was at this level, I hadn't the ability to hold down a job. My concentration and energy levels were way too low for me to function at a normal level. This period of unemployment would last for 6 months.

Employers: the good and the bad

In a couple of jobs, I had to be honest with my employer. I told them I had a bipolar illness. There was a very mixed reaction. We like to think as a society that we accept that there will always be people who suffer with mental illness. From my experience I didn't see that this was always the case. In one job I was told by an employer that the mistakes I was making weren't down to any illness. I wasn't listening to what I was told. He knew someone that was bipolar and fully understood the condition. He obviously didn't and his ignorance was shining through. If, as he proclaimed, he understood the illness, he would have known I hadn't the concentration levels required to take in the information.

One miserable November afternoon I had an appointment with my psychiatrist. They were running late so I was gone from the office for two hours. When I returned, he snapped at me that I cost him €100 due to the fact I did nothing for the day. He had a point, but he was extremely tactless. He ruled his business with an iron fist. He sat across from me and berated every mistake I made. At no stage did he make an allowance that I was having a relapse in my illness. It was a relatively small company. There was no HR department. He told me my performance wasn't acceptable. Two weeks later I left. I couldn't cope with his passive aggression and lack of empathy.

There was one notable exception. I worked in a medical multinational in Galway. I was in a small accounting team of six people. From the beginning, I liked my manager. From a small county Galway town, he had a great way with people. Unfortunately, I would have another depressive episode in this job. I felt bad. I felt I had let him down.

Bosses who have an empathic nature are few and far between. The best always have. When I told this manager about my condition, he was very understanding. He wanted to get as much information on my illness so he could help me in any way he could.

In my opinion, the main difference in what a company is like, is how they treat their employees. If you are missing your targets a poor boss says, "That's two months in a row you haven't hit your targets, if you miss this month's target you're gone". A good boss says "I see you have missed your last two month's targets. What's going on? Is everything okay with you, I'm worried".

From speaking to other people who have had to go on sick leave due to mental illness, overall, employers show very little compassion. In some cases, when an employee returns to work after being off with mental illness, the company effectively terminate the employment through constructive dismissal. This is where an employee resigns because of the employer creating a hostile work environment. The resignation is not truly voluntary.

Companies are now more clued into mental illness. Eighteen per cent of companies in Ireland are now participating in wellness programmes aimed at ensuring their employees look after their mental health. There are companies such as PepTalk (https://www.peptalkhq.com/) that provide these services. This is a positive development. However, there are companies who put such structures in place, so if there is an unfair dismissal on the grounds that an employee has a mental illness, they are covering themselves.

From what I see companies are saying all the right things. However, the reality is profit is king. If you're not increasing the company's revenue, you will not be in their long-term plans. They view you as nothing but a tool, once you are broken, they just throw you away.

In an overall context, considering that I didn't get a diagnosis until 2013, I did well to maintain the level of employment that I did. Whilst you can't put a monetary value on health, roughly over the last 15 years I estimate that my illness has cost me €100,000 in lost earnings.

I have worked through some jobs with severe depression, particularly in 2008. Looking back, I'm not sure how I managed this. I wasn't sleeping or eating properly. I felt at the time that if I went off sick, this would damage my career. I struggled on without medication. I come from a working-class background. From an early age, I was taught the importance of having a job. For the most part this is a positive thing. But I put my job before my own health which was a serious mistake.

As the years passed, it became more difficult to stay in a job when a depressive episode hit. During the recession there wasn't much work out there. I took anything I could get, which was mostly maternity leave contracts. I did manage to hold down two jobs close to home in the years 2014 and 2016. I took no sick days in either position.

It's no coincidence that at the start of both these jobs I took my medication as prescribed. I was well able to work in a productive manner. However, when I stopped taking my medication, the wheels began to fall off. I experienced hypomanic periods six months into both jobs.

Overspending and Peacocking

One of the most common symptoms of mania or hypomania is impulsive and irrational spending. Fortunately, my spending was somewhat curtailed as I hadn't a lot of savings to play with. Most of my money went on clothes I didn't need. Money seemed limitless. I had an insatiable desire to spend money.

I could buy the same jumper in 3 different colours. For some reason, the clothes I bought were always extra colourful. I was decluttering lately, and I found some hideous pink and red jumpers at the bottom of a wardrobe, a fashion crime I had committed in December 2008. I was out to impress. Recently I found a verb that perfectly described my behaviour and why I was lured to bright colours. Peacocking...

Peacocking comes from the behaviour of the bird of the same name. Male peacocks are known to flaunt themselves and their decorative plumage whenever a female peacock is around their immediate vicinity. Behavioural scientists coined the term to describe the flashy behaviour men display whenever there's someone of the opposite sex in the vicinity. I would wear unsightly hillbilly check shirts to stand out from the crowd on a Saturday night out. I was flaunting my wealth that didn't exist. Every clothing item down to my socks were designer. If I met my hypomanic self from late 2008, he's not a person I'd particularly like. At the bottom of all the flash exterior was a desperate need to be liked and insecurities on how I looked.

It also fed into the ideology of grandiosity. I felt I was better than other people. Spending a lot of money on clothes fed into this narrative. I had no issue in going out on my own for a night out. My confidence levels soared. My behaviour, whilst unusual, did make women gravitate towards me. I believe most people are attracted to confident people. It was like a cycle in my hypomanic phase, the more attention I got from the ladies, the more my confidence rose and the more money I spent.

I was relatively old buying my first car at the age of 26. I had learned to drive a few years previously. When I was depressed, I found driving very difficult. I only drove short distances as my concentration wasn't good enough for anything longer than a 10 minutes' drive. When I was high, I had a need for speed and dangerous overtaking. This was probably my most foolish purchase of any episode. It was November 2008. I was nearing the end of my most brash hypomanic episode to date. I was out in Galway with one of the guys I lived with. A friend of his was heading to Australia. He was looking to offload a piece of junk of a car to whoever was gullible enough to buy it. He mentioned in passing to the group, did we know of anyone who was in the market for a bright green 1994 ford fiesta in mint condition? His sarcasm flew past me. Without a thought I said I'd buy it. He wanted €450 for it. I didn't attempt to haggle. I went down to the bank machine and withdrew the money immediately to seal the deal. He was in great form for the rest of the night. Is it any wonder when some clown handed him over €450 without a second thought?

This is the stereotypical behaviour of someone who is hypomanic. Consistently, their decision making leaves a lot to be desired. I hadn't even seen what shape this car was in. I trusted this guy that I had only met 45 minutes previously. In the overall scheme of things €450 for some people in a hypomanic phase would be small pennies. In my case I had €600 to my name, so it was a substantial amount of money. I would live to regret this decision. The car would fail the NCT three times. In the coming months, my mood would spiral into another horrific depression. As my mood was then so low, this brought on a lot of additional stress that I didn't need. A few months later the engine blew on the motorway to Dublin. That was the end of that car.

Some comical incidents arose from overspending. On one occasion I went mad buying pub paraphernalia. Anything from beer mats to prosecco glasses, importing them from anywhere in the world. I bought 16 Peroni pint glasses from a company in England. I was coming down off a medicated high at the time. In my own head I was setting up a mini bar in my house. The only thing my bar would be short of for now were bar stools as they cost too much to ship.

When I came down off my high, I wanted to return 12 glasses back to the seller. Postage was free for returned products. I boxed the glasses and went to the post office to send them back. Of course, I hadn't read the small print correctly. There was no free postage from Ireland. The cost of the postage was more than the value of the glasses. I was stuck with them. Every time I drink from a glass, it reminds me of the hypomanic bedlam that consumed me.

Coming up close to the Christmas holidays in 2008 I had holidays to take from work. I headed to Dublin to splash some cash I didn't have. I sat in a bar in Dublin one Tuesday evening eating a bowl of soup. When I went to pay for it, I realized I hadn't a penny to my name. There was an old Dublin guy sitting beside me drinking a pint of Guinness. He threw me a fiver to cover the soup. I was very thankful. For most people that would have been embarrassing, I didn't feel any that evening.

I was staying with a mate in the city centre. It didn't worry me in the slightest that I hadn't the money to catch a train home. I marched into an AIB bank looking for an overdraft. The girl behind the counter told me I was effectively broke, and it could be a very small overdraft. I was looking for a €1000 overdraft, I was granted a €300 limit. I was fortunate to even get that. It kept me going till the next pay day. Over the next few days, I managed to get a loan of €1000 to cover the car I had bought. I blew it all on clothes.

The overspending was evident in every episode of hypomania. I generally had no more than a €1000 to spend. Luckily for me I hadn't €20,000 in savings, or it would have disappeared. In 2011 I got a credit card which was never going to end well. I maxed out my limit on the credit card of €1100. I would have to be bailed out six months later by a friend. Considering I had a background in accounting it didn't reflect well that I couldn't manage my own finances. Like other aspects of the illness, it was unusual behaviour. Logic or applying it, never arrived in time before there was financial damage done.

Indecision

We are all procrastinators at the best of times. Whether it's a case of fear of failure, laziness or maybe both, it's very unclear. For me when I was severely depressed, my form of procrastination happened due to indecision. The simplest of decisions became very daunting. Routine choices that we all make every day without even a thought I could take an hour to decide. Sometimes I would just put the decision off for another day. The more I put decisions off the harder it became to make any decision.

I would spend a lot of days staring into space when depressed. I'd wonder where it all went wrong. What did I do in a previous life to deserve this horrible debilitating illness? Amid the despair my mind would come up with the idea of having a shower. I could take up to 2 hours deliberating whether to have a shower or not. I know that's hard to comprehend for anyone who has never suffered depression. From speaking to others with depression, the inability to decide on anything is a very common trait of the illness. I think the indecision for my part, was down to anxiety and a lack of confidence to make the correct decision.

I would eventually take the shower which seemed a great ordeal. I think this is an important example of how the illness can impair all levels of functioning. I believe most people aren't aware of the severe cognitive impairment experienced by a person suffering with clinical depression or the low point of bipolar disorder.

I found making a phone call particularly tough and distressing. I would feel completely overwhelmed. What if my voice shivers and the other person becomes aware of my anxiety? What if I can't remember what I actually want to say? All the time my confidence would be dwindling even further down a rabbit hole. "You can't even make a simple phone call, what hope is there for you".

The worst phone calls were when I had to ring work to say I would be off sick for another week. Sometimes they would ask "When will you be back?" which I could never answer. On one occasion I was so anxious about making the call that the nurse had to make the call for me. It could take up to six months or more to be able make decisions promptly again. Along with concentration it would be one of the last things to come back after a depressive episode.

There was no indecision in the hypomania phase; it was the opposite. I decided on a matter without a second thought. There was no time to weigh up the pros and cons of the choice. I was 100% confident when I decided it was the right call. Even if my decision proved to be wrong, I would defend it to the hilt.

Across all facets of my life, I would make poor decisions. I was particularly difficult at work. On one occasion work had gone very quiet. So, I decided to spend half the day on the betting agent, with my boss sitting directly behind me. That was the level of grandiose behaviour I was at. I wouldn't even wait till the boss was away from her table. I would be blatantly on a gambling website knowing only too well that she could see what I was at. I was confronted about it. I got very defensive when she suggested I was half the day online. I remonstrated that I was online for no more than 15 minutes daily. Of course, I was lying. I didn't really understand what the hell her issue was.

That week was when Cheltenham was on. I told everyone I had won €3,000, how impressed they would be I thought. I forgot to tell them I had lost €2,500, so my gambling exploits weren't the outstanding success I made them out to be. My behaviour was very unusual. I was messaging people on Facebook that I hadn't spoken to in over 10 years, enquiring whether they would like me to place bets for them. Poor decision making would yet again lead me to the point of an empty bank account.

CHAPTER 9

Chicago Town

In June 2005, I had just finished my degree in college and was in a hypomanic period. I headed to Galway for the weekend staying with two of the lads.

I was just back from a week's holidays in Fuerteventura. It was my first time abroad. The excitement of my first holiday had further escalated my hypomania. There were four of us on the trip. I slept very little over the week. It was after 3 am every night by the time we came home to the apartment. The less I slept the more momentum my elated mood gained. As always, I rationalised my mood, telling myself that the lovely feeling I had was down to the relief at having finished my degree and the excitement of being abroad. I came home as red as a raspberry. I had drunk for seven nights straight. I always find drinking abroad different than here in Ireland. It's probably the sun or the watered-down vodka, the hangover doesn't get a chance to sink its teeth in.

I would find out to my detriment that drinking a

copious amount of vodka in Galway that weekend would lead me to being carried home by my cousin and his wife. A gang of us went into town just after 7pm on the Friday evening. We stayed in the one bar for the night. Before alcohol took it's hold and still coherent, I approached a brunette standing by the bar. She looked all lonesome. I introduced myself and asked where her mates were. It turned out that she was a 20-year-old lady from Chicago called Emily. I was determined to find out her story. She was on a family holiday with her parents who were sitting in the corner behind us. She was having a few bottles of beer. She wouldn't have had this luxury back in Chicago as she wasn't the legal age of 21. I bought the next round of drinks.

Her dad was burning a hole in the back of my head. She suggested we go to the smoking area to get away from the peering eyes of her dad. We sneaked out without her dad noticing. Neither of us smoked. Within a minute I went in for the kiss. We chatted away for the next few hours under the supervision of her dad. She was going to be in Galway for the next few days, so she asked for my number. She headed off home before midnight and I assumed that was that.

The following afternoon I got a call from a 091 Number. It was Emily. She was wondering where I was heading for the night. She was staying in the Radisson Hotel. I was to meet her at 11.30 pm in the hotel. Her parents would be gone to bed by that time, she said. I rubbed my hypomanic hands in glee.

We hit into town for 9pm. I was preening myself for at least a half an hour. The clock hit 11pm and I walked up to the Radisson. It was a balmy night. I arrived early full of excitement and anticipation

The hotel was quiet. There wasn't much sign of life. I was expecting a wedding, given it was a Saturday night in June. I got myself a bottle of Heineken whilst I waited patiently in the lobby. I was just about recovered from last night's vodka binge so was taking it easy. Next thing Emily came within my sight at the top of the stairs. Jesus, this girl had put in some effort, she was dressed to the nines. Had there been a wedding she would have easily fitted in. We chatted and had a few drinks over the next hour. Mostly chitchat about the Chicago Bulls and how she had met Michael Jordan. I enquired whether her room was nice. Then I received very unwelcome news. She was sharing a room with her parents. Next a surprise development... She suggested a walk of the hotel's five floors. There was still some hope. We eventually came across a storage room full of pillows and duvets. Without a second thought we went in. She was as brazen as me. We spent a while in that pokey little storage room. Not for a second did I think of the repercussions if a hotel staff member had walked in, her sitting on top of me and neither of us wearing nothing but a smile.

That epitomised me when I was in a hypomanic phase. I took sexual risks. I enjoyed the spontaneity of it all. Crazy times, not for a minute, did I think I had an illness. How on earth could you draw a negative connotation from someone who was in top form? Therein lay the crux of this complicated illness. In the words of Ron Burgundy "You stay classy".

Anxiety

Overtime, there was a clear pattern that when the depression hit, my anxiety, like clockwork, always arrived. They were best buddies; one didn't come without the other. When I was high, anxiety was never an issue, it just magically disappeared. From any research papers I have looked at there is a high comorbidity of the two conditions. Research suggests that 50% of people with bipolar disorder also suffer with an anxiety condition, primarily General Anxiety Disorder (White, 2020). When the body is stressed, it produces a hormone called cortisol in large doses. It's the body's way of preparing itself for potentially dangerous or harmful situations. It's toxic. You can't live in emergency mode without consequences for your health.

Anxiety can be the 'primary' problem, or it can be a secondary problem. If it is secondary, it means it is a symptom of another disorder, as it was in my case. Mine was a by-product of a depressive episode in my bipolar illness. I found it to be a very debilitating condition.

My anxiety lasted the same length as my depressive episodes, the last in 2017 being 18 months. My anxiety didn't pounce on me in the middle of the night. It progressed very slowly. I didn't realize it was there, until I was swamped. My stomach was always in knots when I was overwhelmed with anxiety. Every day I had that feeling like five minutes before an interview. My social anxiety rocketed. Even amongst good friends I was incredibly nervous.

I had a few family weddings when both my depression and anxiety were raising their ugly heads. For one of the weddings, I was at the top table. I masked my anxiety well but inside I was a nervous wreck. It was a long painful day smiling for photos. Somehow, I always got through the day.

When my anxiety was at a high level, I found it very difficult to attend any social gathering. I suffered very badly with anticipatory anxiety. The thought of a social event would worry me a month before the social outing. When one worry was over another entered my head automatically. I avoided social events unless necessary.

I know many who suffer with chronic anxiety. It has had a terrible impact on their lives. Such is the extent that I know people who are unable to leave their house. It is one of the leading causes of disability in the world. Like Autism, the condition spans a wide spectrum. I felt at the time that mine was very severe. Fortunately, I never suffered with panic attacks which is a very frightening experience for the sufferer.

It's unfair to judge one's anxiety condition against

another. I have seen one Irish celebrity describe the anxiety she suffers. She would find it difficult to sleep more than three hours in the middle of an episode. Initially I'd have judged her. She can't be suffering with anxiety when she can go on TV discussing it. She has been medicated for periods of up to six months to lessen the impact the anxiety has on her life. So, for her, the anxiety affecting her life is real. It may be different than the way other people experience it but that doesn't make it any easier for her to deal with it.

I'm fortunate that it is not a condition that I have to live with every day of my life. Since I've got my bipolar illness under control, I've had no issues with anxiety. The last three years have been the most anxiety free I have ever been in my life. I don't find the need to take medication to control it. I still suffer a normal bit of anxiety a few minutes before an interview, or if I was giving a presentation. Scientists have now labelled good stress as Eustress. The anticipation of a first date, the first day at a new job, or other exciting firsts also fall under the umbrella of eustress. Eustress is a type of stress that is important for us to have in our lives. Without it, we would become bored and unmotivated.

Concentration

My concentration was gravely skewed, be it a hypomanic or depressive episode. It was the first thing to go and always the last thing to come back.

I'll look at it from a depressive state first. For many years I wasn't clued-in to the early signs of a depressive episode. By the time I noticed it was too late. I was on the floor. Everyone experiences concentration lapses, like the old chestnut of walking into a room and forgetting the reason you walked in. These are just lapses, when the mind is wandering elsewhere.

My lack of concentration was bordering on embarrassing. I could walk into a supermarket and come out five minutes later and not have a clue where I parked the car. I could be in a hotel, and I wouldn't be able to find my way back to the room. As my doctor would say, at my worst I could barely cross the road.

As my confidence dwindled to zero, every one of these concentration lapses left its mark. My internal dialogue would go as follow "My god, you can't even find your way back to your car, how stupid can you get? You're a waste of space".

When you're falling into a severe depression your thoughts become more negative as everyday passes. I tended to be still at work in the early stages of the condition. I was a liability at work, barely recalling what I had done two minutes previously. As to be expected, my standard of work dropped dramatically. At the time I was working in finance where concentration was of paramount importance. Another blow to my confidence, elementary errors everywhere that I couldn't even recall making. The more I fretted about my concentration, the worse it got.

At the time I didn't recognize this was a red flag for impending hell. In hindsight had I notified my doctor at that stage, we probably could have prevented the more severe element of my depression.

On the high swing, my concentration was poor without being quite as bad as a depressive episode. Initially I found at the very beginning of a hypomanic episode my concentration was heightened. When I was elated, I hadn't the time to realize my concentration was waning. Typically, it showed itself up in a huge number of projects started but nothing being near completed. I was hopping from one thing to another.

I could be at work looking at a balance sheet, using Facebook on my phone, sending messages on Plenty of Fish and placing a bet on a Paddy Power app. My productivity was poor. I would be defensive if anyone questioned my work, how dare they, would be my thoughts. My mind was moving so quickly my brain couldn't keep up.

Since I've got well, I have homed in on improving my concentration. There is a monk called Dandapani who I follow on YouTube. He spent ten years in a monastery and is now teaching what he has been taught. He has some interesting theories. He speaks about concentration and how we are never taught as a child how to concentrate. We are told "concentrate on your homework" but never shown how. He sees concentration as a form of art. Concentration is a skill like playing golf or snooker the more you practise the better you get at it He defines concentration as "the ability to keep your awareness on some person or thing for an extended period of time until you make a conscious decision to shift it to something else".

I have followed the advice of Dandapani to improve my level of concentration. With everything I do I solely focus on that one activity. Research suggests that one hour of focused concentration on one concept or idea literally doubles the number of connections in your brain. It might be something as simple as making my bed in the morning. When my mind wanders from what I'm doing I bring my attention back to the activity.

I had a bad habit of not fully finishing activities I started. I now discipline myself to finish the task at hand to the best of my ability. Overtime I have seen a huge improvement in my level of concentration. If I'm listening to someone, I can now really listen to that person without my mind wandering. As a result, I am far more efficient with my time and have become extremely productive.

Awareness is what gives us choice and choice gives us freedom. Emotions are a powerful tool. Controlled and directed they can manifest amazing things. Uncontrolled, they can wreak havoc on your life. We need to look at our mind, body, and emotions as tools. We own them. They don't own us. The brain is a record of the past, it's an artefact. I always dwelled on my problems. When depressed even the simplest of problems seemed unsolvable. Emotions are the end part of past experiences (Dispensa, 2012). I have had to work hard on stopping my brain being a record of the past and focus on the now.

CHAPTER 10

2008 Missed flights

December 2008, I had been high for a couple of months. Life would soon spin into another depressive disorder. At this stage I was not on medication and never had been for any mental health ailment. As the years passed the hypomanic episodes became more intense. Whilst the episodes up until now could be concealed as being an extravert's personality traits, this episode had warning signs written all over it. This would be the first time a few friends suggested all was far from normal.

Lack of organization followed due to poor decision making and lack of concentration. I was to fly over to London for two nights in early December to meet some friends. Even though I was on the breadline, this didn't deter me from going. We had a friend's house to stay in so all I had to worry about was the cost of my flight. I somehow managed to miss flights to and back from London.

My mate John was to pick me up the Friday morning

of the flight outside my house in Castlebar. He warned me to be ready in good time. I was down with a bit of a flu the evening before. I called into a doctor in the town to get some pain medication. My head was all stuffed up. I told her I was heading to London in the morning. She said a glass of brandy might help with the symptoms.

I took the advice. There was a new pub opening that evening in Castlebar. I ventured down on my own. I drank a lot of brandy that evening, a drink I wouldn't be used to. I headed to the chipper afterwards. It was well after 1am when I got to bed. I would pack my bag in the morning.

It was an early morning flight, so John was to pick me up at 7am. I thought I had set an alarm, but it didn't go off. Of course, I slept in, John called he was outside. I hadn't even decided what clothes I was wearing. I took my time packing my bag and grabbed a quick sandwich. I left him sitting outside inexplicably for 30 minutes. On the way out the door, I grabbed a Killers' CD. Rather than apologizing to John, the first thing I did when I sat into his car was to put on the CD. He was rightly annoyed. At this stage we were running very late. My actions would lead to us missing our flight.

I called Knock airport on the way to say we were running late. Would they leave the gates open for another 15 minutes? That was my sense of importance. The plane shouldn't leave the ground until I arrived. Luckily enough there was a flight an hour later going to London albeit another airport. All was not lost. I thought it was a bit of crack really, adding to the weekend. I never apologized. At the time I didn't see the need to. I tried to make out that we were actually better off missing the flight as at least now we had time to grab breakfast. Lucky for me John was a laid-back character, most would have left me in Castlebar.

We spent the two nights on the beer in the city. I never felt so good. The guy that was drowning in depression six months ago was nothing but a distant memory. When I was high, I could never recall how severely depressed I was. In three months', time I would be painfully reminded of the depths of despair I could reach. We survived on a few hours' sleep for the two nights. It would take me another decade to understand that the less I slept, the more my hypomania went into overdrive.

On the Sunday afternoon we were to head back home. We were all hungover so the only person chatting excitedly was myself. There was talk of some of the underground being out of service due to a strike. I was on a laptop checking my Bebo page early in the morning. The cool kids hadn't moved over to Facebook just yet. John asked me to check the website to see what trains were down. I told him all the trains were running as per usual.

We walked down to the underground only to find no trains were running. Again, this was my fault. Even though John asked me to check their website I never did. I was too busy posting up pictures from the weekend. We had to ring one of the lads to bring us to the airport. The traffic was crazy. We arrived too late so yet again had to look for different flights. Fortunately, there was a plane going back to Dublin late that evening. There were two seats left. We booked them, it was either that or wait for a flight back to Knock tomorrow morning. The flights were €100. I had to get a lend from John to cover the full cost.

We had a seven hour wait in the airport. As high as I was that wait did bring me back to ground for a few hours. I spoke to random strangers to pass a few hours. They didn't really speak back but I was too elated to notice that it was a one-way conversation.

On the way down to boarding I managed to leave my boarding pass behind me. I had to sprint back to the check in desk; fortunately, the ticket was still there. Luckily, I had a friend in Dublin where we could crash on the sofa for the night. I had to book the train home for the following morning. I had €50 to my name which covered the train home.

This was stereotypical bipolar behaviour. I ticked all the boxes of the disorder. Very poor judgement and my concentration was beginning to wane. Also refusing to take responsibility for my actions when I was clearly in the wrong. I was very hard work when I was nearing the end of a hypomanic episode. Looking back now, myself and John often laugh about the madness of that weekend. Albeit unknown to me that I was elated, I would pay a huge price to leaving the condition untreated.

Lack of Understanding

I believe most people have a basic understanding of what depression is. People who have not suffered with the illness, can compare it to the feeling they experienced when they were having a few down days. Whilst this is a far cry from clinical depression, at least they have a basic understanding of what people are going through.

The same cannot be said for bipolar illness. Even people who have suffered clinical depression, find it hard to fathom what it may feel like to be hypomanic. I have also met people with bipolar disorder that never fully understand the illness. For many years I was that person.

The crux of the illness is not understanding the devastating effects of leaving a hypomanic episode untreated. Personally, it was such a relief that the depressive episode had finally ended. My depressive episodes were horrific. Every waking minute was agony. For years it never crossed my mind that when I was full of excitement and happiness these feelings were also part of a mental illness.

If the person going through the illness doesn't fully grasp it, how would a person who has never been afflicted understand? There is ample information online, but such is the heavy content, people rarely research the illness. It never occurred to me in the early days before 2013, to even google about the highs.

In comparison to depression, there is very little being done to raise awareness of bipolar disorder. I can imagine being a person who has never experienced the illness trying to rationalise the highs and ending up dumbfounded.

That's the thing, it's not logical. A person may ask: Why on earth would you stay up all night? Why are you not aware that you have spoken non-stop for two hours? All perfectly valid questions. People like to apply logic to any situation. You cannot see the illness which doesn't help when trying to understand it. Recently I have become an ambassador for Aware. They are one of the few Irish mental health charities who bring bipolar illness to the fore of their campaign. It's nice to be involved in a positive project that puts to good use the last 20 years of my life

One of the primary reasons for writing this book is to raise further awareness of the illness. And particularly to explain the different types of bipolar and the highs that come with it.

Krakow and the Salt Mines

A gang of seven of us headed to Poland for three nights on the May bank holiday weekend of 2008. I was living in Castlebar. I had moved into an apartment with two friends a few weeks previously. I had been severely depressed since January. I was following my typical cycle although this time I added fuels to the depressive flames by binge drinking my way through Christmas. I felt at the time that maybe if I moved in with a few friends my depression would ease. It got worse.

It was an early morning flight, so we headed for Dublin airport at 4am on the Friday. Going through the airport felt like hell. Even taking off my belt going through security felt like the biggest of jobs. I hadn't been sleeping at all in the previous the weeks. I had barely enough energy to walk.

It was a three-hour flight. My mind was full of suicidal thoughts, wishing that the plane would crash and take me out of this hell hole. We landed in Krakow around noon. It was very hot. This made me feel weak. I followed the crowd in picking up our bags and heading to get a taxi out to where we were staying, just off the town square.

Of course, we had the best intentions to go sightseeing. As soon as we arrived, pints were ordered. I would drink heavily that day and night just to quieten the suicidal thoughts. Polish beer was strong and it didn't take long for me to get pissed. I was a drunken mess two hours later. I just remember feeling zonked out. As alcohol is a depressant, the following morning I felt even worse.

The next two days just morph into one. It was much of the same, everyone was drinking all day. I drank a few bottles, that was all I could manage. Any chance I got, I went back to the apartment to be on my own. I had thought maybe a holiday away from everything would help things. Unfortunately, my mental illness travelled with me. There was no escaping my sickness.

On the third night, two good mates John and Trev arrived out unexpectedly. These boys knew how to party, they had only been in Krakow two weeks earlier. It helped the night pass a bit more quickly. Trev mentioned to me that I seemed very quiet. I passed it off, I wasn't brave enough to tell him I wished I was dead.

On our final day the boys went drinking again. Two of the other lads who I didn't know that well decided to book a trip to the Salt Mines, a popular tourist attraction an hour's drive away. I would go with them. I had had enough of life. I had decided I'd be going home in a coffin.

It was an hour bus journey. We arrived, to be honest

much of it is a blank. When the mind is busy hatching a suicide plan it doesn't leave room for much else. The mine is 327 meters deep. We were going down to nearly the bottom in makeshift lifts. Every time the tour guide stopped the lift I wanted to jump. Then I thought it would be a mess trying to organize my body home. I would wait till I went back to Castlebar. We returned a few hours later to find the boys where we had left them, boozing. We went for something to eat and drank for the rest of the evening. I sat in silence mostly, thinking how it came to this, that the only answer to my problems was suicide.

We flew back to Dublin on the Monday morning. We arrived home around 6pm. An hour later Fergal headed off to bed. I was left on my own. I would wait till darkness to take my life. I felt relieved it would soon be all over. That was the illness at its worst, convincing you that death was the only answer. There were no alternative options being suggested by my mind.

It saddens me to hear people say that suicide is a selfish act. I can see why people would think that. In most cases the person has died from depression. Their perception of reality is skewed. That reasoned inner voice of what effect it'll have on family and friends is just not there. Like those words do not exist. If anything, I hope this shows that suicides are an extremely tragic event. There is no person to blame.

Darkness fell. The closer I came to deciding the more questions arose. I was going into the unknown. What awaited me when I closed my eyes for the last time? Would it be nothing? Would it be hell for callously taking my own life? At this stage it didn't really matter.

I sat in silence till after midnight. I had knocked the TV off a few hours ago at this stage. The house was quiet, like I was the only person left in the world. I drank some tea, the only vibrations being my heart racing. I had lived the last four months under a constant wave of anxiety. For the last few minutes, my anxiety disappeared. I tried to reflect on my life to see whether there were any good memories. My mind offered none.

I told myself now is the time to be brave. I went up to my room. I grabbed a belt from my jeans and wrapped it around my neck. I pulled at it tightly. My body was in defiance of my suicidal mind. It was like the strength went out of my hand I just couldn't pull that belt hard enough. I threw it away in annoyance. Fine Liam, you're going down to the lake.

At 1am I started the walk. It was a very calm night. There was no cold. An eerie silence accompanied me. I passed a popular pub on the way, Johnny McHale's. Only a few weeks ago I sat in there, drinking pints of Guinness out of desperation to make me sleep. There was no sign of life anywhere. It was a good 20-minute walk, I took my time. As I got to the lake my heart rate increased and then something stopped me...

A story had broken in the local newspapers the previous week. There were reports of people having sex in the bushes beside the lake which was next to a school. It was a serious local issue so much so that guards were patrolling the area a few times a night. I can't walk into that lake, I'll be stopped. Just my luck. I was out of ideas.

I walked home. I reflected how a bizarre story stopped me from going into that lake. It was almost something that would happen to my hypomanic self. Another run in with the cops. I smiled for the first time in months. In a moment of logic, I decided to defer my decision for six months. If things were still hellish, I'd return to the lake. I would see if the summer brought a change in mood. I also thought, you wouldn't know Mayo might go on a good run in the championship. I'd stick around to see. So, the thrill seeking of consensual adults would keep me alive at least for now.

CHAPTER 11

Pablo Escobar

I never dabbled that much in narcotics. The closest I got was taking a then legal high, called wild cat in 2010. Like cocaine it had to be snorted. I took a line but felt no immediate effect. I thought it might be a delayed high, but it never arrived. At the time I was hypomanic so I probably couldn't go much higher than I already was. Coming from Dublin, I brought a bit home for a mate back in Mayo. Even though it was legal I felt on edge going home on the train. He saw a massive effect in that on a Saturday night out he spoke for hours on end, welcome to rapid speech and the hypomanic world.

I was living in Castlebar. Taking cocaine in the late noughties was not seen as a big deal, just a normal part of a night out. Often referred to as "The Devil's dandruff" it's no longer a drug for the rich. It is extremely rare that 100% pure cocaine is found on the streets. Street level cocaine in Ireland is usually around 30%, so as the quality of the product goes down so does the price. The latest I heard you can get a bump for €15.

A weekend wouldn't go by that I wasn't approached for cocaine in hypomanic periods. I rarely went to pubs when I was in a depressive episode. Typically, it was people in their early 20's who approached me looking for coke or pills. Of course, if I didn't take drugs, I wasn't going to go supplying them. People used to get irate when I told them I wasn't some sort of drug mule. O come on we know you have some, you're coked off your head.

Therein lay the problem. When I was approached, I was always in a hypomanic episode. Interestingly, a coke head and a hypomanic head display similar symptoms. Highly arrogant, cocky with a great sense of grandiosity. I'd spot a coke head the second they'd walk into a pub. There was no hiding the effects, it was glaringly obvious. Liam the peacock couldn't hide it either, the only difference being he didn't need to snort cocaine. He produced his high all by himself.

I'm fortunate that I don't have drug addiction problems. When I was trying to get on top of my bipolar disorder, not taking drugs or abusing alcohol made it an easier starting point on the road to recovery. Weed can bring on serious paranoia. A lot of psychiatrists won't treat a patient until they are weed free. With ecstasy, whilst most on the drug are on a love buzz and no harm to anyone, the levels of depression in the aftermath are dangerously high.

I only came across one person I knew who had a heroin addiction, the most harmful of all the drugs. So strong that drug is, that the girl in question was using when she became pregnant. She would go on to have a baby girl who had a hole in her heart because of her addiction. The same girl turned her life around, qualified as a vet and has been drug free the last six years. She does however feel tremendous guilt when she looks at her baby girl.

I'm not sure why as a nation we don't consider alcohol a drug. It affects the brain's chemistry the same way as any of the other illegal drugs do. If alcohol were produced for the first time today it would be the same as other class A drugs, illegal.

My drinking career didn't last long. I used to get seriously depressed after drinking sessions. It didn't take me long to realise this drug wasn't for me. In my eyes it's as dangerous if not more dangerous than other drugs. You lose your inhibitions. Whenever I was suicidal, and I had drink taken my suicidal thoughts were magnified.

Research carried out in America found that about 56 % of individuals with bipolar disorder had experienced drug or alcohol addiction during their lifetime. A large percentage of individuals attempt to self-medicate with drugs and alcohol, to numb the painful symptoms of bipolarity.

Drinking and the use of drugs can trigger a depressive or manic episode. For those with bipolar and drug addiction they will be treated using a dual diagnosis (also known as comorbidity). It's not enough to treat bipolar disorder without addressing the problem of substance abuse, and vice versa. Unless you receive comprehensive care for both conditions, your chances of relapse are high. Relapse prevention strategies for an individual with bipolar disorder must include coping skills for managing the psychological and emotional triggers for substance abuse. One of the main challenges when it comes to dual diagnosis is figuring out where the mental illness stops, and the addiction begins.

There are now facilities that specialize in Dual Diagnosis treatment that understand the overlapping nature of bipolar disorder and substance abuse. As far as I'm aware the only treatment centre for Dual Diagnosis is Saint Patrick's Mental Health Services in Dublin

According to Dual Diagnosis (2021) most mental health services and addiction treatment centres in Ireland are currently not organised to treat such people holistically. Whilst this is not acceptable there is a bill that is in progress to be introduced as of early 2021. "The health (Amendment) (Dual Diagnosis: No Wrong Door) Bill aims to compel the Government to uphold its promise in the programme for Government where it states its intention to Progress the National Clinical Programme for Dual Diagnosis and work to develop joint protocols and referral pathways." (Health Research Board, National Drugs Library, 2012).

Grandiosity

Grandiosity refers to an unrealistic sense of superiority. It's a sustained view of yourself as better than others that causes you to view others as inferior. It is the belief that few others have anything in common with yourself and that you can only be understood by a few or very special people.

This was one of the characteristics of the condition itself that I hated. It always appeared in every hypomanic episode I ever had. It is estimated that around two thirds of people with bipolar disorder will experience grandiosity as some point in their lives (Purse 2019). Personally, I dislike people who think they are better than others. It's not a very attractive trait. When I was hypomanic, I wasn't aware of how pretentious I became. I didn't realise that I spoke down to people. A boss told me once that I spoke down to all my colleagues. It wasn't a nice thing to hear. At the time I wasn't aware of my behaviour.

Grandiosity appears in other conditions as well. It is a feature of Narcissistic and anti-social personality disorders. However, grandiosity tends to be more aggressive in bipolar disorder than other illnesses. The presence of grandiosity is used in combination with other hypomanic symptoms to confirm a diagnosis of bipolar disorder.

Grandiosity can be difficult to pin down, as it can come across as arrogance and boastfulness. The condition can present itself in other ways, as well such as:

- Exaggerating your own achievements
- Criticizing and dismissing other's achievements or talents
- Believing yourself to be infallible
- Believing that you are more intelligent than others
- Being quick to anger if you are challenged
- Being unable to see how unrealistic your beliefs and actions are.

Like most aspects of bipolar disorder there were always consequences for my behaviour. People around me didn't understand that the symptoms were a result of a bipolar II condition. I came across as unforgivably conceited and rude. It affected all my relationships, be they with friends or work colleagues. My sense of judgement and social norms had disappeared.

Grandiosity never occurred in my depressive episodes. Since I have become stable, I have had no symptoms of the condition. As with rapid speech, the symptom was put under control with mood stabilizing drugs. Thankfully, I have seen the back of this distasteful symptom.

On the face of it, grandiosity could be mistaken for self-confidence. I see that there is one key difference. Confidence is being at a place that you don't worry what people think of you. Grandiosity is trying too hard to make out that you are superior to most people.

Selfishness bordering Narcissism

Since I've been well, I've had time to reflect on the last 20 years. It's funny, as time passes by, sometimes I forget about the severity of the illness. Part of me thinks things couldn't have been that bad. On the other hand, my last depressive episode which spanned 20 months reminds me that they were. I could see why anyone would think I was self-obsessed. The illness really does consume you.

In hypomanic episodes I displayed signs of being a narcissist asshole. I had an extremely high level of my own importance. I constantly desired admiration from others. I didn't take criticism at all well. One symptom I didn't display whilst hypomanic was lack of empathy for others. Even in periods of hypomania I always understood people going through pain. If anything, I always wanted to help.

Other similar symptoms included setting high unattainable goals and very impulsive behaviour. Now that I am stable, I know that I'm not a narcissist. I only presented signs of narcissism during hypomania. A bit like the key difference between hyper sexuality and sex addiction, to have a narcissistic disorder one needs to display these symptoms on a continued daily basis. Mine were very cyclical, generally for five months every year coinciding with the hypomanic periods. Once I returned to a depressive state and retreated into my shell, the feelings of grandiosity and the quest for admiration were but a distant memory.

When you're recovering from a depressive episode in bipolar, one of the biggest challenges is finding energy to do anything. The main aim for the first two months in recovery was eating regular meals and getting back into a sleeping routine. Even the process of lifting a fork was tiresome. It took energy to fully open my mouth to eat. Due to the extreme lack of energy my whole body slowed down.

This is where it gets tricky if you have a partner or kids. There is little energy left for your loved ones. It was like the life was drained out of me. I hadn't the energy to muster up a conversation and if I did, I didn't believe there was anything that was worth talking about. It's here where relationships begin to crack. The lack of energy can be perceived as taking your partner for granted, that you are selfish and uncaring and put your illness before the relationship. It effectively ended two of my relationships, albeit they were both in the early stages.

It was almost a Catch 22 situation. To be able to maintain a relationship with your partner long term, you have to put yourself first to fully recover. However, if as in my case, an episode lasted 20 months, this was a long time prioritizing yourself. I always felt I was fortunate not to have kids when I was trying to get on top of my illness. If my partner were left holding the baby, I can only imagine the guilt I'd feel. If your partner is left in this situation, you can see why the relationship could end overnight. As with most aspects of the disorder, there is no quick fix.

There certainly was an element of emotional drive-by that went on in my earlier relapses. It was 2013 before I really engaged with the mental health services. Before that it was friends and family who I dumped all my problems on.

I did see counsellors time and again, but I always stopped going in the manic phases. The option wouldn't be there to go back when the inevitable depression kicked in. No doubt it was arduous to the untrained person who had to listen to me. My cousin was been the first person I confided in 2009 that I felt something was wrong. He encouraged me to see a GP. For the next three years he was the first person I visited to inform him that the depression was back. He was level-headed and had a good general understanding of mental illness.

Eventually I would get myself well again or what I thought was well. I tended not to want to reflect on the depressive episode. As far as I was concerned it never happened. This was a serious lack of insight on my behalf. These episodes were happening every year, surely it was something I needed to at least reflect on to prevent another episode. The obvious reason was, there was never a period of wellness, I went straight into another hypomanic episode. The only concern I had was how far I had to travel for my next Plenty of Fish date.

I didn't reflect that my cousin had to absorb a lot of my negativity for six or seven months at a go. It didn't occur to me to call him in the aftermath to thank him for being there at my beck and call. Narcissism had already kicked in; that phone call never happened. Hopefully, he's reading this, and I'd like to thank him now.

It was best for all parties when I came under the care of a mental health team in Claremorris. I'd imagine it frightens most people when you tell them you'd rather be dead. When talking to professionals I could tell them how bleak things had become, without putting worry on family members.

Skyfall

There's an old proverb "See Naples and Die", meaning once you have seen Naples one can die peacefully, since nothing else can match its beauty. In September 2011 another onset of severe depression loomed. A company I worked for in Galway was wound up, so I had to move home. The depression was gathering pace. By the beginning of October, I was fully immersed in another uninvited episode.

I saw that Naples proverb in the context of a Lonely Planet's review of the magnificent cliffs of Moher. I had never been. I had heard that this was a suicide hotspot. I read a couple of articles online about the harrowing details of the shape a body was found in after the 700 feet plunge. It was never a case that you only hit the water; most peoples' bodies shattered against the rough rocks on the way down. Sometimes it took weeks to recover a body, particularly in bad weather. Some of the lost souls are never recovered.

The more I thought about it one Friday evening, I felt it could be a poignant way to end my life. I sat on my thoughts for a few weeks. I tended to do that when depressed, spending an eternity to decide. Every week that passed the depression further emaciated my body. At this stage I had so many depressive relapses that I felt this would be my lot for the rest of my life.

I felt there was no longer hope of me ever making a full recovery.

I woke up on Halloween morning which had fallen on the bank holiday Monday. I had been out for a few drinks the night before. A few friends from Dublin were down for the weekend. At this stage I had told nobody bar close family about my mental illness. So I put on the best mask I had. I had zero interest in being there. I thought it might give me a bit of a pickup; it had the opposite effect. I had to get out of the house, I didn't feel like interacting with anyone. I sat in my car with no real idea where I was heading. I decided to drive Galway direction.

About 10 minutes into my drive, I decided the Cliffs of Moher was the only destination worthwhile. A sense of calmness came over me. This would be the end of my relentless pain. I hadn't the energy to withstand another nine-month recovery. It was a horrible afternoon; the rain pelted the car windscreen. I took a turnoff for the cliffs, my heart rate increased. I parked up. From reading about cases of suicide at this beautiful place, the general theme was a person travelled alone and left a suicide note in their abandoned car. I found it very hard to write anything when I was this depressed.

I paid in. I walked slowly towards the cliffs. I was surprised how busy it was considering the time of year and weather. It was full of tourists. I could hear the American accents as I climbed the steps to the highest point. To prevent people from falling there was a fence. If you stayed on the official route, there was no chance of an accident occurring. I carefully climbed over the low fence.

I looked below to see the waves bashing against the jaded rocks. It would be a 700-foot fall till I hit water. I came close to the edge. My legs shook uncontrollably as the magnitude of what I was going to do swept my mind. I tried to push myself forward, but my body rebelled. Once again, I had balked. How the hell was I going to get out of this world? I climbed back into safety and slowly walked down to ground level. I returned to my car and sat there in silence for over an hour. I drove home once again pondering another failed attempt.

Since I've been well, I have returned to the cliffs. My failed suicide attempt is something I have never told a soul. It serves as a stark reminder as to how ill I had been, but also how fortunate I am to be alive today.

CHAPTER 12

Jacinta the Promiscuous Hen

I bring you back to August 2008. I was mid-twenties and as high as a kite. My illness was generally seasonal. My mood would usually rocket in the summer months. A good mate Fergal and I hit for a Saturday night out in Galway. We moved between several pubs, finally settling in the Dail bar. When we walked in, I spotted the infamous plastic willy and a group of ladies. A sure sign that there was a hen party. Fergal warned me not to bother going over to talk to them, as my chances of having any success with any woman in the group were slim.

I paid no heed to him. I was full of grandiosity at the time, so I went for the hens headfirst. I got chatting to one of them at the bar and managed a kiss. Jacinta from Kerry, a lovely girl. They were down for the weekend. Jacinta told me the wedding was only two weeks away. So, we were sitting on a windowsill outside kissing when the rest of the hen party came out. There were a few yelps "good on ya Jacinta, enjoy yourself". A bit strange, I thought

I asked Jacinta so

Where is the hen

In the biggest Kerry accent

What do you mean like, I am the hen.

As she flashed the engagement ring. O balls, I've shifted the hen! I genuinely didn't know she was the hen. Not in a million years would I think a woman to be married in two weeks, would have been on the lookout for some fun.

So, my barrage of questions began.

Do you not feel guilty?

What would your hubby think?

She blanked me. Ah this isn't right, if you were my fiancée and I found out you'd be gone. She laughed as she pulled me along.

We're walking up shop street.

Let's find a hotel.

She ran to a bouncer outside the Meyrick asked how much it was to stay, €200 euro at least, he reckoned. She wanted me to foot the bill, no way.

How could you turn me down it's my last night of freedom before I marry?

Even if I wanted to, I didn't have the cash. She priced The Radisson, the same price. It was an August bank holiday weekend. Nowhere around the city centre would be less than €200. She had to settle for Supermac's and a burger meal.

We got our chips. At this stage she was still pissed off, so the conversation had dried up. I had lost Fergal at this stage. I was staying at a mate's house just outside the city. She was staying in a B&B with a few of the hens out the same direction. We queued for the taxi. As we were sharing a bag of chips, I could see her texts popping up on her phone one text came up - Enjoy yourself Hun xxx,

Who's that from?

O that's my aunty.

I was speechless. The taxi arrived. Thankfully, it was a short enough journey as it had got a bit awkward. She slammed the door and walked off. There was no goodbye. I filled the taxi driver in, he was in stitches. That was the last I saw of Kerry's Jacinta.

How does Bipolar affect the Brain?

Before I had a full understanding of bipolarity, I simply blamed myself for the condition. It was a result of lack of mental toughness. I had failed at life. The reality is bipolar is a complex illness caused by changes and variation in the brain. They were changes I couldn't possibly have prevented. I was not to blame. It wasn't something I had asked for.

Chemical imbalance is listed as one of the main causes of the illness. The brain is a chemical factory that makes chemical messengers called neurotransmitters that regulate mood 24 hours a day. The main chemicals are dopamine, serotonin, and noradrenaline. There's some evidence that if there's an imbalance in the levels of one or more neurotransmitters, a person may develop some symptoms of bipolar disorder. Increased dopamine activity is associated with mania (and psychosis). In contrast, decreased serotonin and noradrenaline activity are associated with major depression and may also have a role in the depressed episodes of bipolar disorder.

One part of the brain that the experts agree is affected is the Amygdala. This is deep inside the brain. It is the emotional fragment of the brain. The amygdala alerts us to fear, it responds to things that are rewarding, and is also the seat of aggression. It identifies the things in our environment that are emotionally important to us.

If a fire is ignited near us, we see danger. In a bipolar person that alarm is multiplied. If we see something rewarding, like a bar of chocolate, a fragrant flower, or the sweet smile of a baby, the amygdala lights up. We feel a flush of pleasure. If you have bipolar disorder, the response of the amygdala is exaggerated, and you may feel that reward with far more intensity. Many mood-stabilising drugs used to treat bipolar disorder are known to decrease the excitatory actions.

On the other side of the spectrum when the amygdala is turned down, we have no emotion. This makes sense to me. When I was depressed, I felt no emotion. If the whole of Ballyhaunis had been blown up it wouldn't have sparked an emotion. I wouldn't be able to cry.

Basically, the amygdala activates far more emotion in people with bipolar disorder than it does in other people. So, you feel those emotional reactions with more intensity and understandably, you're likely to express those emotions with more intensity too. There is evidence that the amygdala in children with the condition is smaller than normal.

Another part of the brain that is affected is the frontal lobe. This is the part of your brain that makes decisions. It also makes you think about what you're doing. This area helps with mood regulation and helps us inhibit behaviours we may feel like doing but know are not socially advantageous to display. In a bipolar brain the frontal lobe simply does not do its job. When someone is manic, they have no brakes in the frontal lobe, but the amygdala is red hot. When someone is in a depressed state, think the opposite. The frontal lobe is turned all the way up everything has just stopped, nothing is getting out. There is also highly stimulated aggression without the inhibition to control it.

Another part of the brain that seems to be affected is the hippocampus. This part of the brain is used for processing all long-term memory and emotional responses. In patients with bipolar disorder there seems to be a decrease in volume.

Poor behaviour is the result of altered areas of the brain that heighten emotion, when the brain is lacking the equipment it needs to manage emotional responses.

Energy

This is where the contrast between the two different sides of the illness for me, were at its most vast. I'll first look at it from a depressive perspective. In retrospect my dip in mood began three months before a full relapse. Like my concentration, my energy gradually waned over time. I would begin to feel tired all the time. Next up would be aches and pains in my body. Every episode tended to follow the same sequence

When the full relapse took hold, my body effectively shut down. It could barely move. To walk for five minutes would feel like climbing Croagh Patrick. In a sense this is where confusion lies on the difference between clinical and mild depression. In no way are they comparable. It's like comparing a paper cut to losing feeling in your right arm.

Most people are aware of the positive connotations associated with running and feelings of wellness. Without doubt, running out in the fresh air can prove an antidote to mild or even at times moderate depression. The major thing here is the person has the energy to go out for a run. When clinically depressed, that's not an option. Climbing the stairs is an ordeal.

There is a pop psychologist in us all. People mean well by giving advice on the benefits of exercise for your mental wellbeing. When the body is in shut down mode, going out for a run is a long way down the tracks. Obviously, people in the fitness industry push the positive mental health benefits strongly. The downside to this is you have the public believing that no matter what the mental health issue, exercise is the answer. I know from personal experience that exercise alone will never keep my bipolar disorder under control. There needs to be an honest conversation about the difference between mental health and mental illness. We all have mental health, but we don't all have mental illness. Exercise will cure that sluggish and tired feeling you get from sitting on the couch all day. Mental illness is different. This is a health condition the same as diabetes is. Most of us with mental illness will require medication or talk therapy, or in my own case both.

On the flip side of the coin, we have hypomania which brings an abundance of energy. It is not a normal energetic spurt that most people experience on a Friday looking forward to the weekend. There is no major need for eight hours sleep, I'd easily manage with five hours. I would have various projects on the go. I couldn't be wasting eight hours sleeping. Coming from an all-time energy slump to a high sustained level of energy was a welcome relief. When energy was at its peak, I felt I could operate on only a few hours' sleep.

My energy levels always coincided with my two annual

mood distortions. Both episodes took their toll on my body. In the hypomanic phase I would eventually get to a point of a burnout. The things I focused my energy on were rarely productive. So, whilst I felt I was getting so many things done, the reality was I ended up with ten projects most not even half finished.

As with concentration, I have zoned in on how I use my energy day to day. I have realised that like money, it is a finite resource. I only have so much. I am careful with whom and on what I use my energy. I have noticed in hypomanic periods I had too many people in my life by my own accord. I would be contacting people on Facebook, that I wouldn't meet from one year to the next.

There are certain people who fill me with energy and those that drain me. They are called energy vampires (Dandapani, 2017). There is a distinction between temporary and inherent energy vampires. A temporary energy vampire is a person going through a difficult phase in their life. You find them draining but you know this is just a phase, so you are happy to support them. An inherently energy vampire is this way all their lives. It is a personality trait. I try not to get involved in deep conversations with these people, just some chit chat about the weather. I try to choose wisely who I have meaningful conversations with. When I walk away from a positive conversation, I feel uplifted. This maintains my energy levels.

Circadian Rhythm and Sleeping pills

Circadian rhythm is basically a 24-hour internal clock that is running in the background of your brain. It cycles between sleepiness and alertness at regular intervals. It is often called the Sleep/Wake cycle. It is common for people who suffer with bipolarity to have a poor sleep pattern. I was no different.

Unmedicated episodes of depression lead to nights upon nights of broken sleep. Long term insomnia on its own is debilitating. With insomnia you're never really asleep and you're never really awake. Whatever chance one has of recovering, regular sleep is the starting point. From the hypomania viewpoint, a lack of sleep made me more manic.

It wasn't until 2013 that I turned to sleeping pills. I hadn't slept for days so I was prescribed two sleeping tablets to be taken at night-time. That night I took the tablets as prescribed. They knocked me out to such an extent I was barely able to walk up the stairs. I then proceeded to fall in the bathroom, nearly splitting my head in the process. The next time I woke it was morning. It's hard enough to describe the quality of sleep I got off the pills. I did feel less tired than if I hadn't slept. It still didn't feel like a natural induced sleep. I tended to wake up with a very similar feeling of a hangover after drinking ten pints the night before. Still, it was the best option I had at the time. Sleeping pills were never a long-term solution. Their job was to try and regulate my circadian rhythm, to aid better sleep in the long run. I would reduce to one sleeping tablet in the coming weeks.

Whilst depressed I'd spend 10 hours in bed. I pushed myself to get up at this stage even though every part of my body wanted to just lie there. Hypomania had the opposite effect. Five hours' sleep would suffice. I was too busy to be bothered about sleep. I never had an issue going to sleep but would wake up a few hours later full of beans.

It goes without saying at this stage I should have been on medication to ease my highs and get my eight hours sleep. One medication I took after the sleeping pills really helped my sleep. I took Seroquel to level me out, to stop the high periods of bipolar illness. During any episode Seroquel really aided my sleep. It had the added benefit of not feeling hung over the next day. There was a feeling of grogginess the following morning, but a cup of coffee and a light jog have minimised the symptoms.

Seroquel is a drug that has a dual purpose for me, it controls the highs and aids sleep. This is one of the medications I will be on probably for the rest of life. I know if I miss a dose at night-time, I find it very difficult to nod off to sleep. I wake up very unrested the following morning. As my body has got used to the medication, the sedative effect has substantially reduced but still is enough to aid a good night's sleep.

Since I've been well, I have focused in on my sleep hygiene to maximise the quality of sleep I am getting. A similar but more systematic approach to better sleep is Stimulus Control Therapy (SCT).

Stimulus Control Therapy

This involves ensuring that the bed is only associated with sleeping. The goal is to strengthen (or re-establish) the link between the bed and sleep and to weaken the learned association between the bed and activities other than sleep including wakefulness, worry, fear, frustration, and anxiety (Runko, 2009). Patients are advised to get up after 20 minutes if they are unable to sleep, to do something relaxing until they feel drowsy and try again. If you still can't sleep, the advice is to get up again and repeat the process.

A part of your hypothalamus (a portion of your brain) controls your circadian rhythm. Outside factors like lightness and darkness can also impact it. When it's dark at night, your eyes send a signal to the hypothalamus that it's time to feel tired. Your brain, in turn, sends a signal to your body to release melatonin, which makes your body tired. That's why your circadian rhythm tends to coincide with the cycle of daytime and night-time (and why it's so hard for shift workers to sleep during the day and stay awake at night).

Your circadian rhythm works best when you have regular sleep habits, like going to bed at night and waking up in the morning around the same time daily (including weekends). I have implemented this into my sleep routine. I get up at 7.30 am seven days a week. I was never an early bird, so it was difficult at first, but it's become habitual now. I tend to wake up ten minutes before the alarm clock. I have a more sustained level of energy now throughout the day.

I'm not quite as strict with the time I go to bed. I know I need about eight hours' sleep to be able to function the next day. So, bedtime is now between 11-11.30 pm. I am acutely aware if I'm up looking at a possible project at 2am that it's a red warning sign of an impending hypomanic episode. Like the waking up before the alarm I can feel the tiredness coming on after 10.30pm. I now have a bedtime routine that I implement an hour before I go to sleep.

My phone is one addiction I struggle badly with. I put it out of my grasp in the last hour of the day. I take a warm shower. I watch some light TV that my brain doesn't have to engage too much with. Engaging in the same or similar activities at the end of the day will signal to your brain that the day is coming to an end and its almost time for bed. Since I have implemented this daily routine, I have seen excellent results. I used struggle drifting off to sleep, now I fall asleep within 15 minutes and sleep through the night.

When I sleep well it has a very positive domino effect. I can start my day with a 20-minute run. I make healthy food choices. I don't need a dose of sugar to give me a jolt. I also find my brain is sharper and more alert ensuring I make good decisions throughout the day. From someone who was an insomniac, I never dreamt I would get to a level of being a very efficient sleeper.

CHAPTER 13

Not All Heroes Wear capes

July 2012 - I was in full flight. When I was elated, the dates came thick and fast. Most were non-events. We went for a drink, cue awkward silences and the famous easy out phrase "I didn't feel any spark". On one occasion for a first date, I brought a lady out for dinner in a fancy restaurant in Galway city. This was an excruciating experience, five minutes in, it was dead in the water. The big problem was that we had ordered the starters at that stage. We got on like a house on fire online. The conversation was free flowing but come the dinner date we struggled to make basic conversation. Neither of us suggested we meet up again.

I got talking to one girl who was on the outskirts of Galway city. She was a single mum with a six-month-old baby. She seemed nice. She said she found it difficult to get babysitters so asked would I like to call over to the house to watch a DVD on Saturday evening, I agreed. There was no sexual innuendo, so I was expecting to watch a film. This lady had a different plan in store.

As I was getting ready, I got a request for an explicit photo. I declined and said that I would be over in the next half an hour. Her house was at the back of a very quiet housing estate. As I got closer to the house, I noticed the front door was open. As I approached the front door, I soon become aware that we were playing out this woman's sexual fantasy.

I'll try and explain what she was wearing. Knee high leather boots, a thong, and a see-through lace top with a noticeable absence of a bra. I thought to myself, not all heroes wear capes. For once I was speechless. Her bedroom was the first room on the left. As I approached to say hello, she stood at the entrance to the bedroom. This, even for, me was nuts. I tried to normalise the situation by saying, "Will we have a cup of tea first?" to which she swiftly responded. "Do you not want to go to bed." The tea and digestives were delayed.

Later in the evening we would chill and watch some TV. Her baby boy of six months was now awake. An adorable little guy. His dad was not involved. I felt a little sorry for her, as she told me he won't even answer her phone calls.

The following morning, she asked me, "If you had a son from a one-night stand would you walk away?"

My response was no, I'd face the consequences of my actions as I was responsible for the outcome. I did find it an unusual question to someone she had just met. I left soon after. I dropped her a text a couple of days later. Her response was, "Sorry I don't know who you are." I hoped that she reconciled with the father of her child. I had been used. My circus would plough on.

Bipolar and recurring behaviours

Looking back these repetitive behaviours should have been glaringly obvious. At the time, it never occurred to me that I was slipping back into old ways, the hypomanic trends. I was completely oblivious.

The depressive episodes year after year reared their ugly heads in the same manner. For whatever reason I never intervened quickly enough to prevent a full-blown depressive episode. I always left it to when suicidal thoughts took over. At times, captain hindsight comes to mind. Imagine if I had got treatment in my early 20's. I would have saved myself a decade of impending hell. If I never had tinkered with my medication, my 30's would have been plain sailing.

The signs were very subtle at first. Tiredness would be the first thing to kick in. I would attribute this solely to work. At this stage I tended to buy multi-vitamins to give me a pep. Next up were early stages of social withdrawal. I'm quite good when it comes to keeping in contact with friends. Most of the time the communication method would be by WhatsApp. Suddenly, I would disappear from this medium. Over time my friends became very aware of this. They could see the relapse coming before I did.

At this stage, the depression was gathering momentum. Poor concentration would follow. I would have to double check everything I did, even the smallest of things like locking the door. I often would have to turn around and drive home to see whether I had locked the front door. Next, I would find myself waking up with no enthusiasm for the day ahead. All I could think of was that I couldn't wait to get back to bed.

My sense of taste would disappear, food tasted so bland. Every day that passed I got steadily worse. The next few symptoms all came together. My anxiety went through the roof. Everything now was a worry. I was lucky if I got three hours sleep. My appetite went completely. I started losing weight at an alarming rate. Finally, I became overcome with suicidal thoughts. A few weeks later I would pay a visit to my doctor but at this stage the damage was done.

My early hypomanic behaviours were extremely subtle. They were practically the flip side of the depressive behaviours. At the beginning there were the smallest changes in behaviour. One being that I would curse a lot more. A simple little thing was evidence of a change in the tide. Almost overnight I had an abundance of energy. I wanted to organize a meet up with any friend I ever had. I could have twenty unanswered messages in a WhatsApp group but kept typing. At this stage, my social media use went off the charts. My newsfeeds lit up with music videos I liked. It didn't matter that I spent a lot of the day at work updating my social media profiles. I would have very tangential speech. I began to spend a bit more money on things I didn't need, mostly clothes.

Next, online dating would take over my life with an abundance of dates. A couple of months down the road I would become cranky and irritable. Now I realize that this was the last point at which I should have intervened to prevent the hypomanic episode causing untold damage. I never intervened. Every day that passed I was beginning to wreak havoc at work and in friendships I had built up. At this stage, the depressive symptoms began to kick in. From the age of 22 onwards on every occasion this is how my mood disorder played out.

One Flew Over the Cuckoo's Nest

Electroconvulsive therapy (ECT) is a procedure, done under general anaesthesia, in which small electric currents are passed through the brain, intentionally triggering a brief seizure. (Waite and Easton, 2013). ECT seems to cause changes in brain chemistry that can quickly reverse symptoms of certain mental health conditions. There is research that shows it can help both the depressive and manic state of bipolar disorder. It is mainly used to treat the depressive phase of bipolar disorder.

There's a famous film 'One Flew Over the Cuckoo Nest' starring Jack Nicholson. He plays a convict who faked insanity so he could avoid hard labour in prison. He was admitted to a psychiatric hospital and part of his treatment was ECT. I watched the film recently and my stomach feels queasy watching the ECT scenes. His body shook violently whilst four people held him down. The scenes are so horrific it's hard to think that ECT is humane.

Cinematic depictions of mental illness have profound and lasting implications in the real world. It is widely acknowledged within psychiatry that One Flew Over the Cuckoo's Nest led to inappropriate levels of suspicion and misinformation regarding ECT. It may have meant many people did not receive treatment that is proven and effective. All this due to a single film's misinformed presentation.

This isn't something the professionals suggested for me whilst on my path to recovery. I was aware of the treatment and to be honest it was something that scared me. I would never have considered it as an option. That fear was borne out of lack of knowledge.

The treatment today is far more humane. It is given under general anaesthetic with muscle relaxants, so the body does not convulse during the seizure like it was depicted in the film. No-one is entirely sure how it works, but it is thought to change the way brain cells interact in parts of the brain involved in depression.

In my time in the psychiatric centre, I met one gentleman who had ECT administered on him. We became quite friendly, so he spoke very candidly about his experience. He had tried all the other conventional treatments to treat his severe depression in the previous three years. Nothing was giving him any relief from his symptoms. He reluctantly agreed to a session of ECT. He said he experienced no pain. He did find it helped his symptoms. I was surprised to hear that it would be part of his long-term maintenance treatment. He had got eight sessions in a four month period. As is a widely recognized side effect he did suffer short term memory loss. He explained it in the context of when he woke up, he had no memory of the road to travel to get home. After a few weeks, his memory did return. I haven't spoken to him recently, but I do hope it was successful for him.

The jury is out on the effectiveness of the treatment. I have spoken to professionals who advocate for the treatment as a last resort, when all other treatment options have been unsuccessful. In their experience, there has been a very high success rate on patients recovering from their depression and preventing future manic episodes. It doesn't have a 100% success rate but neither

does any treatment for mental illness. It's often been compared to chemotherapy. Like ECT, chemo doesn't work for all patients, or they may need several sessions to reap the benefits. ECT is still used quite widely today. I've no doubt if I hadn't come out of my last 18-month episode, ECT would have been a serious option that I would eventually have to consider.

Lightbulb moments

These occurred quite frequently when I was well into a hypomanic episode. These could range from setting up an online dating company to buying online stock and selling it on as a profit. I became a Del boy character, "This time next year Rodney, we will be millionaires". I was fully sure I would live the dream of the rich and famous. I felt I was destined for great things. Many of my ideas were only pipe dreams. I told my friends what I had planned on doing but never took any serious steps to implement the ideas.

One of my quirkier ideas was to find a way to beat the bookies in every horse race. Many a person has studied the form, but this was far from an exact science. I was looking for a bullet proof way to guarantee I won something on every race.

As I come from an accounting background, I was very familiar with spreadsheets and Excel. I began to concoct a plan to put a small bet on each horse thus guaranteeing a win of sorts. All I needed to do was figure out how much of a stake to put on each horse. This is where Excel came into play. All I had do was to change the odds and the number of horse racing.

I concluded that the best races to back, were ones where there were even horses and the odds for a few of the horses were 14/1. Don't ask me how I came to that conclusion. I calculated roughly that I could win €5 on each race. So, if I backed twenty races a day, I would have €700 at the end of the week, as a top up to my normal wages. It really was wishful thinking.

I told a couple of mates of mine, so we decided to test run it on a Tuesday night. I was as high as a kite, they played along. I never got the figures to work in a way that made a profit. I was still adamant that I had hit gold. We stayed up till four o' clock in the morning doing up different permutations. It was too late to go back to Galway, so I stayed at my friends for the night. The plan was we would all test it out on a race the following afternoon. I stayed overnight. To my annoyance the next day the two boys were working and didn't answer the phone to trial my new plan.

At the time I had a very bad flu. I had made an appointment with my G.P. for 9am that morning. It was nearly afternoon before I arrived expecting to be seen; a complete sense of grandiosity and entitlement. My GP rightly told me to come back the following day. When we met the next day, I took ten minutes explaining my madcap idea. I believe he was hoping that I would show some insight into the fact I was in a hypomanic episode. That didn't happen. I was too busy with my new project.

To this day my doctor and I still discuss that extremely flawed idea borne out of a highly elated mood. It's another good example of what it's like to be hypomanic. Crazy times.

CHAPTER 14

Cattle break

Early 2011 and I was well on my way to another hypomanic blowout. I was living in Galway. I started conversing with a girl from Ballinasloe called Rebecca, online. She seemed quite nice. We had a phone call before our first date. The conversation was dominated by talk of her last ex-boyfriend. She was out of a nine-year relationship a few weeks earlier. I figured it was quite normal to be still irate about the breakup considering it was so recent. She had been dumped and it was clear she was still getting over it.

We organized a date for the following Tuesday. I would go down to meet her in Ballinasloe around 10pm and we'd go for a few drinks. I arrived down in good time. I parked up at Tesco and rang Rebecca. Three times it rang out. She had stood me up. There was no point letting the evening go to waste, so I did the week's shopping.

Twenty minutes later, as I was about to pull out of the car park. my phone rang. It was Rebecca. I had barely answered the phone.

I'm so sorry are you still in Ballinasloe? I got delayed.

No problem I'm still here.

I'll be there in 15 minutes.

Excellent, it wasn't a wasted trip after all. In my mind, this girl was dressing up to the nines, thus explaining her running late. I hadn't gone to any great effort myself. I just hoped I wasn't way under dressed. Fifteen minutes later she pulled up in her brand-new red golf. She hopped into my car. We had an awkward kiss on the cheek.

Will we go for a spin? I'm sorry again for being late.

There's no need to be sorry I know you can lose the run of time when you're getting ready.

O no it only took me 10 minutes to get ready. A few of my cattle broke out, I had trouble getting them back into the shed.

I started laughing, this girl had a good sense of humour. She wasn't laughing though. You couldn't make it up. I had nearly been stood up because of a few Friesian cattle. We spoke about farming for the next ten minutes. I hadn't a clue what she was on about. I don't come from a farming background. In fairness to her it was more than a few, twenty of her cattle had broken out. She was real country.

After our farming lesson, she went on to speak about

her ex-boyfriend again in great detail. We drove around Ballinasloe aimlessly. This was a disaster. I wasn't getting a word in, which was an achievement considering I was in rapid speech mode. I didn't know Ballinasloe that well, so she was giving me directions.

She brought me down a bog road unintentionally. There was nowhere to turn so I had to back into a bog to try and get out. The wheels starting spinning. Christ! Don't tell me I'll have to call out breakdown assist in the middle of a bog in Ballinasloe. I just about got out. At this stage it was half eleven all the pubs were closed.

Rebecca asked me how I thought the date was going. I took the easy out and said I didn't think there was much of a spark, so we drove back to the car park. We left it at that. About the only good thing that came out of that date, was a funny story for the lads.

Alexander the Great

When I was in the early stages of a hypomanic period, I wanted to be a friend to all men. It didn't matter whether I knew a person for a few days, I treated them the same as a friend of ten years. This caused issues as I knew no boundaries. I had lost the art of how to socially interact with people that I didn't know. I had no filters.

In October 2009 I started a twelve-week contract job in retail that would bring me up to Christmas. I was at the beginning of a hypomanic period. I had never worked in retail before, but as it was the early stages of an episode, I came across as a confident outgoing person which were the perfect attributes for this job

I was eager to make friends. As the weeks passed, my behaviour started to get more erratic. I felt I had great connections with all the people I worked with. I was only working with them for little over a month so it couldn't have been the case. I was very outspoken at lunch and wanted to know everybody's plans for the weekend if there was a gang going out together. This must have been very uncomfortable for the people I worked with. I don't believe they thought that I was mentally unwell, just probably extremely pushy and arrogant. I hinted at dates with a few of the girls. I didn't care that I was flirting with several of them on any given day.

For one guy, I stepped on his toes once too often. I asked him whether he knew if any of these girls were in relationships to which he said he wasn't sure. Then I asked him if he would mind finding out. I didn't want to be wasting my time talking to girls who already had boyfriends. He got annoyed and said "I don't know you or don't want to get to know you, so stop asking me questions". I put this down to him being an asshole. In my view I was only being friendly, and he was a guy with issues. When I look back, I'm a bit embarrassed, even though there was no serious damage done. It was almost a biproduct of rapid speech. I had a lot on my mind, so someone was going to have to put up with me.

One of the girls I was flirting with was from Macedonia. I wasn't aware she had a brother who also worked there. He told me in no uncertain terms that I wasn't to flirt with his sister. I didn't take much notice of him. It was harmless stuff, so I didn't know what his issue was. I continued flirting. One day I was working he pulled me aside. "If you talk to my sister again, I'll break your legs". This struck a chord with me. By his demeanour and bulked up body, this time I took him seriously. I backed off immediately. A few weeks later I felt the storm had blown over. As I was pulling in for petrol my buddy was coming out of the shop. He pointed to the cameras. "The next time I meet you, there won't be any cameras. I'm going to break your legs". He had a friend along with him who looked equally aggressive. I had a bad feeling about this guy. I decided to tell the guards, after all it was already a verbal assault. They would do a check on him. He had previous assault charges against him and had been in prison previously. The guards pulled him in and warned him to back off. He did so for a few months. It was mostly verbal abuse after that. When he met me on the street he started shouting and roaring at me hoping to get a reaction. Thankfully, he moved on from the West of Ireland a few years' back.

Had I brought this on myself? I suppose to a certain extent I had. If I had backed off after the first warning, it probably wouldn't have escalated to the level it did. I tended to attract aggressive people when I was in the latter stages of a hypomanic period. At that stage I was also aggressive, so wasn't fazed by confrontations. I was a little unlucky that this woman's brother was a convicted criminal.

As the weeks passed by, I became more and more grandiose. When I was in this mood, I had absolutely no respect for any authority. I would talk back to any manager who crossed me. This didn't go down well in particular in this job. I was warned by one of the senior bosses that I was walking a thin line. Frankly, I didn't really give a toss.

Toxic People and Recovery

Most family and friends have the best intentions when supporting someone who is recovering from any mental illness. However, this doesn't always mean they say or act in a way that is helpful.

I don't believe most people understand how serious the illness is. In my case it was 50/50 whether I'd still be alive the following day. I found it difficult to articulate how ill I was in these periods. I said very little when I was getting professional help. If they knew it was a life-or-death situation, I believe they'd be more careful in the way they acted. Yet I didn't feel it was fair to put the magnitude of the situation on them. These periods stretched anywhere between six and twenty months. There was nothing to be gained by having someone on tenterhooks for such a long period.

A common theme I found was that some people believed that my depression was very selective. When I was recovering, these words felt like daggers in the heart. In one instance I heard people saying, "How could he be depressed when he's able to go to a Mayo match yet he's not able to go and do a day's work". It was cruel to be this ill and have people question the legitimacy of your condition. Trust me, no one would invite this illness into their life voluntarily.

The gap in knowledge on mental illness is seismic. This time I confronted the two people on talking about me behind my back, which I felt I was well within my rights to do. Their response was very hurtful. One proclaimed "Someone with depression is a person who isn't able to leave the house". He said it with such confidence that it appeared he worked in the mental health field. Pop psychology at its best, god knows where this guy picked up that nugget of information.

When I was severely depressed, there was no day that I felt like leaving the house, but I did so anyway. To stay in the house all day would be feeding the illness. On the accusation of selective depression and going to a football game, this was ignorance personified. It could take me a few weeks to muster up the energy to go to the game. I'd be full of dread and worry. I wouldn't be able to draw much enjoyment out of the game. However, as a marker in overall recovery this would be a huge steppingstone.

To be able to mix with others and manage the anxiety of the whole event was huge. Yet there were people belittling this stepping-stone by throwing a huge negative spin on it. Why aren't you back to work? There is nothing wrong with you. Going from attending a football match to going back to work for 40 hours a week was more than a stretch. If my energy was sapped after a minor social outing, how would I cope a few days later being fully focused on work for a full week?

This is something I really feel the need to take to task. If I were unfortunate enough to get cancer, I don't believe there'd be questions about the illness being selective. If I attended a social occasion there'd be a warm welcome with the positive message that it's great that you were able to make it. Yet this level of empathy does not exist for another illness in the body. People suggest that you're weak, unmotivated and downright lazy. On one occasion I was called a loser by a neighbour. When in the throes of depression, a comment like this can bring improvement to a shuttering halt. So, what's the best approach if you have toxic people in your life?

Hanging around the wrong people can thwart your recovery. It's hard to feel good about the day when you're including negative and dysfunctional people. In some cases, it can prevent you from recovering at all. We owe it to ourselves to walk in the direction of peace.

I was rightly told by the professionals to surround myself with positive individuals as much as possible. In the back of my mind, I thought that I was the most negative person of all to be around. Why would people be prepared to spend time with me? When in this vicious circle your self-worth is at an all-time low. It was hard to understand why anyone would bother. Here's what I found helpful in dealing with toxic people.

- Remove the person from your life. If this is not possible don't allow these people space in your life.
- Put up an imaginary stop sign in your head. It sounds very basic. I use it when there are too many negative thoughts coming into my mind, but also when people are making snide comments.
- React with compassion. When someone attacks or questions whether you have an illness in the first place, the initial reaction is to match fire with fire. I think like most people with bipolar illness, I am a sensitive creature who always feels exhausted after a row. In the past few months, I've developed a strategy to overcome these challenges. I use a visual technique in where I see the person as a child so react with a sense of compassion. I find my response is a lot calmer when using this visual technique.
- Be brutally honest when someone takes a cheap shot. I carefully phrase my response to these accusations. I let the person know that they've hurt my feelings and ask them to explain where that thought pattern came from.

We need to be careful that we don't start playing the victim. After all we choose who we want to hang out with. There's a great saying "Some people in your life are there for a reason other are there for a season". It's very important to recognize when people's seasons are over.

CHAPTER 15

Living with someone with bipolar illness

I have never had personal experience of living with someone with bipolar disorder or any other serious mental illness. I was always in the opposite corner. In one of my relationships the girl suffered with depression, but it was well under control. I can only imagine the difficulty, when you finally thought you had seen the back of the illness, up turns a manic episode. Relationships and your life are turned upside down once more.

I imagine you're constantly on guard, looking for cues of an impending episode. It must be exasperating to be on tenterhooks even in periods of stability. There's a book called 'To Walk on Eggshells" (Johnston, 2006) which is a story of a mother who is caring for her daughter who has bipolar illness. She speaks about tiptoeing around her daughter's issues and dare not upset her for fear of making things worse. I've no doubt this book would resonate with any family who is caring for someone with a mental illness.

I think sometimes parents blame themselves for what has happened to their child. Was there something they could have done differently? In most cases the illness would have appeared regardless of the environment the child grew up in. Your behaviour as a parent is not solely responsible for their bipolar illness. There is probably a chemical imbalance from day one with the illness usually appearing in the teenage years. From speaking to others who were caring for someone with a mental illness, they felt a huge responsibility being a caregiver. They spoke of being emotionally and physically drained.

Studies have shown there is a high incidence of carers developing depression due to the mental strain of being a care giver (Central Statistics Office, 2021). My longest depressive episode was 20 months. I was fortunate I had access to excellent mental health services. I'm certain that whilst there was still a level of strain on my partner and family, it was of some solace that I was under professional care. Until 2013, the strain was all on my family. There is a sense of helplessness. I know the illness inside out. When the illness is at its most frightening there's very little family members can do.

I'm sure there are feelings of resentment towards the partner or family member, but this is an illness the same as any physical illness. No human would choose to have this illness. They already feel guilty that they are a burden on their family. A high majority of people with bipolar disorder stabilize overtime and live a normal life. Whilst the temptation might be there to walk away, if you can muster the energy to last the course your partner/family member will in time recover.

There is so much information online now. It can make it less daunting to deal with your sick family member. From the perspective of having the illness, sometimes the best thing family can do is just to be there. It maybe that the person doesn't want to talk. Having the presence of someone in the room is a support in itself.

Routine and IPSRT (Interpersonal and Social Rhythm Therapy)

A friend said to me recently how important maintaining a routine is for him. Over time I have learned that to keep my sickness at bay, routine is imperative. I have spoken earlier about the importance of keeping our circadian rhythm (sleep/awake cycle) consistent every day of the week.

In the last six months I have discovered there is an actual therapy whose sole focus is helping a patient to maintain a helpful routine in their lives. Interpersonal and Social Rhythm Therapy (IPSRT) is a specific type of psychotherapy developed to help people with bipolar disorder.

IPSRT was designed to directly address the major pathways to recurrence in bipolar disorder, namely medication non-adherence, stressful life events, and disruptions in social rhythms (Frank, 2007). It is an evidence-based treatment. Research has shown that it is effective in helping patients manage life who have a mood disorder (Black, 2021).

It focuses on helping people to identify and maintain the regular routines of everyday life. It is founded on the belief that disruptions to our routines and sleep deprivation may cause or exacerbate the symptoms of the illness. When studied as an adjunctive treatment for bipolar disorder, IPSRT gave patients a significantly longer time before the occurrence of a new episode. Participants in IPSRT also showed improved occupational functioning. When studied during bipolar disorder trials, IPSRT patients had a shorter time to recover from episodes than patients outside the control group.

Unbeknownst to me I have been following this form of therapy. I do keep my sleep, eating and exercise schedules the same daily. Black, 2021 says IPSRT is incredibly helpful for people with bipolar disorder. This form of therapy focuses on stabilizing a person's daily rhythms.

The "social rhythm" part of IPSRT centres on creating a daily routine that a person can stick to long-term. People with bipolar disorder tend to live less regimented lives. They may not go to bed at a reasonable time, they may eat sporadically. Adding normal times and a schedule to these things can help them take control of their condition.

Employment is very beneficial to those with bipolar as it makes it so much easier to keep a routine, five days a week. I have found this to be the case in my situation. I have to work a lot harder to keep a routine when I'm unemployed. It takes discipline to get up in the morning at the same time as if you were leaving the house to do a day's work. Once I got myself well, it took me about six months to establish a firm routine as I hadn't been working. It has now become automatic not to consider hitting the snooze button on the alarm.

This type of set routine has a positive impact on your circadian rhythm (the collection of physiological processes timed to light and darkness that you go through over the course of 24 hours). This interplay is important because your circadian rhythm influences so many aspects of how your mind and body function. The release of hormones can influence your mood. As with most therapies you must keep a mood diary. This makes it easier to identify what routines are helpful. Also, it increases the chances you can avoid another episode. It is also why getting regular sleep is an especially crucial part of IPSRT. Since your circadian rhythm and sleep habits are inextricably intertwined, it's no surprise that poor sleep can trigger manic and depressive episodes in people with bipolarity.

This therapy is combined with psychiatric medication to keep bipolar symptoms at bay. There is no evidence to suggest that IPSRT on its own can help a person with bipolar to be episode free. Like most therapies it doesn't work for everyone. For those people who do respond, most have seen a reduction in the symptoms associated with bipolar disorder.

CHAPTER 16

Preventing relapses

Over the last year, I've worked hard to gain as much knowledge as possible to reduce relapses. As mentioned earlier in the book sticking to your medication is the fundamental building block. There are additional things that can be done to stay well.

- Logging your mood - It was recommended to me by my psychiatrist to write down how my mood was for the day before I went to sleep. Research suggests the effect that journaling has on depression is profound (Weingus, 2019). Reflecting on your emotions at the end of the day in a journal is cathartic. In the morning, I read over what I had written the previous night. The main benefit was that I could spot the early warning signs such as lack of concentration and being passive aggressive towards people. Anytime I felt like coming off my medication I would take my journal out as evidence of all my past episodes.
- Exercise - 20 minutes a day, preferably outdoors

- Don't lie in bed ruminating - Negative thoughts will always win. Put your foot on the floor and move. Once you start moving, have a wash and eat something, you have already won the day.
- Become self-aware of damaging behaviour - I tend to have repetitive unhelpful behaviour that signposts an episode. I would become obsessed about how I looked, particularly when it came to my skin and body weight. Becoming self-aware of damaging behaviour and challenging the negative thoughts behind this, can be of great help.
- Appoint a few friends as spotters - If I were becoming hypomanic my friends would see the warning signs before I did. A simple phone call could be telling in whether I was at the beginning of another episode. If there was an impending depressive episode my voice would be filled with anxiety. I also would want to get off the phone as quickly as possible. At the other end of the spectrum, I could stay on the phone all evening.
- Talk therapy - There are a lot of options here, anything from C.B.T to counselling to psychotherapy, to name but a few. It may take a while to find a therapy that suits you best. I wound persist at looking at all talk therapy options till you find one that you find beneficial. For some people this means being in counselling for the rest of your life. Personally, for the time being, I have finished

with talk therapy. I've done a huge amount over the last 10 years. This isn't to say that I wouldn't return to talk therapy in the future.

- Make time for yourself and acknowledge how you are feeling - This hectic world doesn't allow much time for slowing down and thinking about emotions, so you have to make the time (Lipton, 2005). It is your responsibility to try and carve out a meaningful life.

- Manage your relationships - When I was in a hypomanic phase I could say things that would really damage a relationship. I have learned overtime to apologise and address what I said to the other person. I found if you don't, these things accumulate. This approach can protect relationships.

- Arguments- Not every argument is worth winning. At times, it is ego driven that one must have the final say. I find that I tend to feel harder than most people. Whilst externally I might not show any signs of sensitivity, I find a full-blown argument leaves me upset and stressed.

- Work Stress- If you become overburdened with work this can push you up through the gears. The mind won't allow a bipolar person to shout stop. If people who are prone to highs, the stimulus of the pressure shoots them up.

- Fixed Routines - Try to eat your meals at regular hours. As mentioned earlier keep a regular sleep routine. If you want a relapse "stay awake".

Supermarket Sweep

The countdown was on to Christmas 2011. I was amidst another debilitating depression. I was back living at home in Ballyhaunis. I was doing a bit of shopping in Lidl on a Friday evening which was the day before Christmas Eve. There was a giddiness in the air as most people were finishing up work for Christmas. I always found when depressed, Christmas really drove home how bad things had become. There was a girl I went to school with ahead of me in the queue. I really wasn't in the mood for chit chat, but I didn't want to come across as ignorant either. I hadn't seen this girl in years. I asked how everything was going. She gave me a short brief; she was happy with her lot.

She asked me how I was getting on. That day I just didn't feel like lying, "To be honest Nora, things are crap. I'm in bad health, I've no job and don't have a penny to my name." She had just put her last item through the checkout. She looked at me very genuinely and said, "Liam that's fantastic you're doing so well."

I was fit to strangle her. She hadn't listened to a word I said. What could I say, only nod? On the drive home I was bitching away about her in my head. I bumped into that girl recently on the street and we said hello. It got me thinking back to that afternoon in 2011. However, this time I was observing the situation from a positive mind set. That evening my mind was set on negative overdrive. There was no room for reasoning.

What I failed to register that day was how things looked from her point of view. Firstly, she had two young toddlers who were a handful and both fighting with each other. Secondly, she had just run up shopping that was close to €150. In all fairness, she had enough going on without wondering how a fella was doing, that she hadn't seen in 10 years.

There was no malice in this situation, just the reality of life. Everyone has enough going on without worrying about others. In ways when I look back, there was a good lesson to be taken from Lidl that day. The reality is apart from family and a few close friends, nobody really has time to be concerned about your life situation or health concerns. So, the "What will people think?" question is a pointless one to ask, as most people won't be thinking about you either way.

There's great comfort to be drawn out of this. If one of the reasons you are afraid of getting treatment for your mental health illness is based on what others will think, you can rest assured as you won't be crossing their mind. Perspective is everything.

There's a great quote from a prominent French poet in the 1960's Anais Nin: "We don't see things how they are; we see things as we are." The older I get the more I see that statement to be true.

Bad Cops

In August 2005, not long out of college I got offered an accountancy job in Galway. I was a few months into a hypomanic phase. I didn't know a soul down there which didn't bother me. When I was high, I was in my element meeting new people.

In my new house there were three others, two doctors and a police officer. The doctors were very friendly. I didn't see too much of them as they worked 48 hours shifts a lot. The police officer was not so pleasant. I didn't like him from the moment I met him. He was very stand-offish. One of the doctors mentioned in passing that they felt the same way as myself.

When I was high, I was oblivious to social norms. I could be very inconsiderate of others. On this occasion I was playing the radio full blast at 7.30 am every morning. One evening I came home to find the lead of the radio was gone. Straight away I suspected the cop. I'd leave it a day to see if he would return it. No sign a day later. I went into his room to try and find it. There it was, thrown in the corner. Such an ignorant thing to do. He could have just asked me to turn it down like most people. Not that I would have listened.

The next morning, I turned up the radio even louder. That evening the lead was gone again. I went straight up to his room to get it. This time he had left a baseball bat on his bed clearly for me to see. The lead was under the bed so again I took it. The next morning it was gone again only this time around I couldn't find it in his room.

What a prick! I wasn't giving up easily. He had an Xbox in the sitting room and the lead would work my radio. So, I began to use it. From now on before I went to work, I would hide the lead in my room. I continued this for the next few weeks, the radio blaring every morning without fail. One evening when I came in, the radio was gone. The bollix had taken it. I never saw it again. I was livid. I still held on to the Xbox lead and bought a new radio. I was being very petulant. I moved out shortly after that so there was never an altercation.

I was difficult to deal with when I was hypomanic. I just rubbed a lot of people up the wrong way. I had another incident with the Gardaí. Back in spring 2011 in another hypomanic period I had to call to the guards to get an electorate form filled in. I called into the Castlebar garda station. There was no one at the front desk. There was a sign saying to buzz the buzzer once and wait for someone to come out. As always, I was impatient. I put my finger on the buzzer for a good 20 seconds. One of the guards came running out and took the head off me. What was his problem I thought? That summed up my lack of consideration for others.

CHAPTER 17

The Nomad

Between the years 2009 and 2013 I lived in twelve different houses. The lads used to call me the Nomad. I never settled for more than a few months anywhere I lived. Now in four of those cases I had to move home as I wasn't well enough to work. In a lot of cases during hypomanic episodes I was told to leave. I felt I was in no way to blame. I had become a nightmare to live with.

The more manic I was, the bigger the fallouts. In 2010 I was particularly troublesome getting kicked out of two houses in the space of three months. My only defence would be that these were owner occupied houses. I'd learn over time that this was always a recipe for disaster. You never felt it was your home. They all used to proclaim at the start, "It's as much your house as it is mine." This was never the case. In that space of time, I lived in four owner occupied houses.

Whilst manic I lived in my own world. I had a reduced need for sleep. I would generally be up till 3 am every night. The telly would be loud. Not for a second did I think of the other people in the house, who had to be up at 7am in the morning. One Tuesday morning in the middle of the night in January 2010, I was listening to some AC/DC and cooking chips in the kitchen. To further add to the noise, I had the dishwasher and the washing machine on at the same time. I heard the landlord thundering down the stairs. He pulled the plug on the dishwasher, washing machine and radio in the space of five seconds. Thankfully, he didn't turn off the chip pan or there would have been a row.

He didn't say a word and stormed back to bed. What a knob, I thought. I usually pay my rent on time. I'm entitled to do whatever I want in the house. The following day he told me his ex-girlfriend and child were moving in on Friday. He wanted me gone by the weekend. I was only in the house six weeks until I was given my P45. In my own head I felt I was as well off; this fella was zero crack. By Saturday I had found another house a few doors up from where I was.

Another owner-occupied house, this wasn't a particularly long stay either. We got off to a bad start. I didn't have the full deposit. I would pay it in dribs and drabs over the coming weeks. In all houses I lived in, tea bags and milk were generally for anyone in the house. I was told off very quickly not to be taking her tea bags. Considering I was quite high this was never going to work. I was shaving one morning, and the sink was blocked. So, I took a cup out of her cupboard. It didn't help that it was one of her best china cups. I didn't have the sense to leave it back without her noticing. I left a plastic razor in it. Later that evening she found her china cup. She went nuts. I had at least the sense to half apologize. I still blamed her. If the sink wasn't blocked, I wouldn't have had to borrow a cup.

I told her that a girlfriend of mine was coming to stay for two nights. She had no issue with this initially. She changed her tune very quickly. On the second night, she said my girlfriend owed money for the ESB she was using. Now she was acting petulantly at this stage. I think it was her way of saying, I want you gone. The next day I packed my stuff and left. I texted her to say I had moved out. She replied with one word "fine". I would move home then for a few months. As per usual three months later I was seriously depressed. This depressive episode would last six months which was relatively short by my standards.

By Christmas time I was running into another manic episode. I had got another job in Castlebar and decided to move down. There wasn't that much accommodation available with it being bang in the middle of the college year. Students had taken the nicer houses. I swore I would never move into an owner-occupied house again. Unfortunately, I had no other choice, such was the lack of accommodation. As in my previous experiences, this would also be short lived.

The trouble started when I was cooking steak on a Saturday evening. As was normal when hypomanic my concentration and memory were poor. I headed off to a friend's house without thinking of turning the oven hob off. It never crossed my mind. Luckily, the owner was in the house, or it could have burnt down. I returned Sunday evening to his wrath. He rightly went down my throat. This was more unfortunate than anything. I always did things like this when I was in the midst of an episode. On one occasion I forgot to pull the handbrake up on my car. I got up the next morning to see my car 50 yards from where it was parked.

There was no coming back from that. It turned very sour after that. He pulled me on everything from leaving a bread knife out to not putting on the dish washer. The writing was on the wall. I found somewhere else quickly after that. The common denominator in all these incidents was me. My behaviour was erratic to say the least. I was a loose cannon. Looking back, I wouldn't have wanted to live with someone that behaved like I did now. I was a nightmare.

My next house was more of the same. This time I moved in with a couple and their dog. This was another bad move. Living with a couple was always going to be overbearing. Poor decision making was a constant theme in my Nomad days. I was specifically told not to feed their dog as he was extra sensitive to food. He was on a very strict diet. Of course, any evening I was having my dinner I fed him the scraps even though they warned me not to. I was a law unto myself.

This ended in a big row with the gentleman in question. There was tension between us now in the house. They decided to get another dog. They never informed me, so I was pissed off. I thought it was ignorant. The first I saw of the puppy was when I came home one evening and he was underneath the stairs. They had gotten a gate to lock him in as they were gone away for the night. He barked through the night. I was raging. I left a post-it on the fridge that I wanted the dog gone. This led to a full-blown row the next evening culminating in the guy grabbing me by my neck. This stay lasted three weeks and that was that.

Every house I lived in I left a trail of destruction behind me. I never thought for a second, I wasn't well. As far as I was concerned the world seemed to be against me. It was nothing but bad luck. My bad behaviour ended after that incident. The three houses I lived in Galway after that I got on fine, making a good few friends on the way. Sadly, on all those three occasions I would get seriously depressed having eventually to move home.

Wellness

At the time of writing, I am over two years in good health. For the first time in 25 years, I have not had a depressive or hypomanic period. It seems unusual to have gone this long without an episode. It had become normal to be amidst another episode. It's of no coincidence that it's the first time I have taken my medication as instructed long term. No missed doses or second guessing my psychiatrist's recommended dosage by cutting tablets in halves or quarters. Whilst there are still plenty of challenges ongoing in my life, I feel far more capable now of dealing with these issues.

I feel I have my life under control. I'm in unchartered territory. I've never had more knowledge about the condition. I feel I am a step ahead of the illness for the first time. Every day at the end of the evening I reflect on my mood and how I interacted with people.

Does this mean I have seen my last relapse in my condition? That's a question I will never be able to answer. Evidence would suggest that people who stick to their medication, significantly reduce the risk of having reoccurring episodes. If I do come off my medication, history suggests I'm almost guaranteed to have a hypomanic episode followed a few months later by a severe depressive episode. Medication holds the illness in check. When you stop taking medication you're playing with death. Although medication remains one of the primary treatments for bipolar disorder, research has shown that regardless of the drug regimen, medication alone is not enough to prevent relapses (Helmer, 2019).

It's a question I ask myself most days. Would a relapse be as severe as an episode triggered by coming off medication? The experts say you can never say that someone with bipolar disorder has had their last episode. Relapse is part of the illness. Relapse is self-perpetuating. Once it happens, the more likely it is to happen again.

It's possible to do all of the right things, follow a proper medication regimen, eat well, exercise, minimize stress and get enough sleep and still experience relapse. Unfortunately, there is no clear understanding of why this happens.

The experts suggest that a patient with bipolar illness type II diagnosis is up to 14 times more likely to relapse than someone with a bipolar type I diagnosis. Personally, I believe the key is to be highly vigilant to any slight change in mood and treat them both as potentially hazardous.

I'm at a stage of wellness now that I am in control of the illness to a certain extent I have taken responsibility for my treatment plan, taking my medication as prescribed. I also ensure regular exercise, good diet, and sleep. As I have gotten older, I realize the impact my relapses have on my family and partner. I owe it to them to do everything possible to stay well, whilst at the same time acknowledging that a future relapse may be outside of my control.

Turning the tide

As a nurse said to me recently not everyone has had the success and good fortune of overcoming their bipolar illness as I have. For every person that keeps their illness at bay, there is another individual who has been haunted their whole life by the condition.

Many ask me, how after 20 years of suffering that suddenly, the penny dropped. Was it just one simple thing that was a game changer? At times I feel that it is a very straight forward answer. Taking my medication as prescribed was the solution after two horrid decades. On reflection it's a complicated illness, not one thing alone turned the tide. Adherence to medication is one piece of a maintenance treatment jigsaw.

As a starting point I had to try to understand the illness. After my diagnosis in 2013, it would really take me five years to get to grips with it. Coming off medication was the clearest indicator of my lack of insight and knowledge. It wasn't until I got well in the Autumn of 2018 that I began to study the illness in depth. This would prove an invaluable exercise.

I studied it as if I were sitting an exam the following day. I soon realized that my health will never be owned, it's rented, and the rent is due every day. I have continued this for the last two years and hopefully every day going forward. There is no longer an air of complacency. I realize that there is always the possibility of a relapse. I want to be always one step ahead of the illness. I have prepared myself as much as possible if a relapse arrives.

Writing this book has allowed me the opportunity to continually research the disorder. Not a week goes by that I don't add to my knowledge bank. Rather than making the illness an enemy, I have embraced it with open arms. I've stopped running away from my condition.

In the past I wanted to forget all the depressive episodes. This is no longer the case. I now realize there is learning to be gained from each episode. They are in the back of my mind, as a reminder of when unwatched, my bipolarity will rip me to shreds. I've begun to take responsibility for my illness. I know a medical team is there as a support, but I work hard to manage my condition by myself. As I write I've been discharged from the mental health services in Claremorris. This is the most pivotal day in my life since I got my diagnosis in April 2013. All parties involved believe that I am now well-equipped to manage my illness.

I am super vigilant of how I live my life. Yes, I take my medication, but I have also become a watcher of my behaviour. Are my thoughts beginning to race? Am I aware that my anxiety levels are very high? Has my sleep routine fallen akilter?

I am still quite hard on myself, but in a positive way. I berate myself if I feel at the end of the day my life isn't any better than the day before. At times I still feel resentment towards people who questioned the validity of my mental illness. When depressed these words were like daggers to the soul. After years of attacks, I now realize that hanging onto the resentment is the equivalent of letting someone I dislike living rent free in my mind. My resentment is like bacteria; it breeds and grows and leaves me feeling not myself.

For years I lost so much time to rumination and to what purpose? Rather than focusing on recovery I was wasting my energy on futile thoughts leading to me feeling drained in many ways.

Every few weeks I still must challenge these thoughts. All it takes is some quiet introspection for the realization that these people spoke out of lack of knowledge. They will always hold the same opinion. No amount of me stewing over their callous words will change that. They moved on quickly and so should I. I am no longer a prisoner of others' opinions. I have a newfound freedom to focus on what I love in life with good health been to the fore.

End Game

I no longer feel shame or stigma for having the illness. I have made peace with it. I have no issue in accepting that I will have to take medication for the rest of my life. I now actually see taking the medication as the easiest thing to do to keep my condition in check. I have educated myself about the illness and continually do so. My friends and family are aware of the illness. My WhatsApp group will see the symptoms if I don't.

It is such a good feeling waking up not dreading the day ahead. Don't get me wrong, I'm not doing cartwheels at 7am either. It's a normal mood. The day ahead isn't that exciting, but it almost seems a distant memory that I would rather be dead than face the day ahead.

I don't have the rush of ideas that I had when I was high. Ideas do come, but not at the same rate. These days I am more likely to put an idea into practice. I logically think things through. Is this idea a pipe dream or can I put steps in place to make things happen? I have a newfound clarity in life. I can focus on the task in hand. There is no jumping between tasks and getting none of them completed. I am more present when people are talking to me. I don't interrupt a person mid-sentence.

I have a confidence about myself. I don't feel the need to compare myself against others. I focus on improving myself every day and being the best me. I have learned to be more assertive, which has taken time. In all the years being depressed, assertiveness had disappeared completely. I won't be pressured into something that I know will have a negative impact on my condition.

My sense of humour has returned even now, in a pandemic. I can stand back and still enjoy parts of my life. I accept there will always be challenges, but I can put things into perspective. Money might be extremely tight. A transition in careers might not be as smooth as I would have hoped but I'm in the best mental health of my life.

I've been able to articulate the last 20 years into a book. I've found writing very therapeutic. It's something I could never have imagined doing up to two years ago. It almost feels like closure for the last 20 years. Every experience I've had I've discussed. All my thoughts are now on paper. I feel satisfaction that I have completed a project that has been ongoing for over two years. From a person who championed in procrastination to a person who has developed discipline to complete a long-term project. From a talk therapy point of view, I can draw a line under it for now.

I feel pride that I fought the good fight over the last 20 years. So many times, I wanted to throw in the towel, but something deep down made me keep going. Most of all I feel very lucky. Very few get the chance to tell their story. Too many tragically die, never realizing help was available that it didn't need to end up like this.

I wouldn't wish the illness on my worst enemy. Am I a better man for coming out the other side? Absolutely. Anyone reading who is in the midst of despair "It will pass". You will grow through what you go through. Stick in there for now. There is a life worth living out there for you. Be brave and reach out to someone who will pull you out of the abyss.

REFERENCES

Beck J, (2011) *Cognitive Behaviour Therapy Basics and Beyond.* Second Edition, New York, The Guilford Press

Black R, (2021) *Treatments for Bipolar Disorder: Cognitive Behavioural Therapy and More* Available at https://www.psycom.net/bipolar-psychosocial-treatment Accessed 04 July 2021

Brazier Y, (2018) *What are suicidal thoughts*, Available at https://www.medicalnewstoday.com/kc/suicidal-thoughts-ideation-193026, Accessed 08 September 2019

Central Statistics Office (2021) *Irish Health Survey 2019- Carers and Social Supports*, Available at https://www.cso.ie/en/releasesandpublications/ep/p-ihsc/irishhealthsurvey2019-carersandsocialsupports/carers/ Accessed 12 July 2021

Dandapani, (2017), *Self-worth and letting go of guilt*, 13 November. Available at https://dandapani.org/blog/self-worth-letting-go-guilt/, Accessed 09 November 2019

Dispenza J, (2012) *Breaking the habit of being yourself*, London, Hay House Inc.

Dual Diagnosis Ireland (2021) *Dual Diagnosis Ireland*, Available at: https://www.dualdiagnosis.ie/ Accessed 29th July 2021

Judd LL, Akiskal HS, Schettler PJ, Endicott J, Maser J, Solomon DA, (2002), *The long-term natural history of the weekly symptomatic status of bipolar I disorder. Archives of General Psychiatry,* Available at https://www.ncbi.nlm.nih.gov/books/NBK545957/, Accessed 22 March 2019

Frank E, (2007) *Treating Bipolar Disorder a Clinicians Guide to Interpersonal and Social Rhythm Therapy,* New York, Guilford Publications

Gillian P, (2017) *Mental Health a Stubborn Stigma*, Available at :https://www.irishtimes.com/opinion/editorial/mental-health-a-stubborn-stigma-1.3214196, Accessed 15 September 2019

Health Research Board National Drugs Library (2018) *Dail Eireann debate. Health (Amendment) (Dual Diagnosis: No Wrong Door) Bill 2021: First Stage.* Available at: https://www.drugsandalcohol.ie/33708/ Accessed 21st July 2021

Helmer J, (2019*) Bipolar Disorder and dealing with Relapse* Available at https://www.bphope.com/a-bumpy-road/ Accessed 05 July 2021

Johnston J, (2006) *To Walk on Eggshells*, Helensburgh Scotland, The Cairn

Lauren B, Snezana U, Abramson L, Hyman S, Nusslock R, Whitehouse W, Hogan M, (2011) *Progression along the Bipolar Spectrum: A Longitudinal Study of Predictors of Conversion from Bipolar Spectrum Conditions to Bipolar I and II Disorders* Available at https://www.ncbi.nlm.nih.gov/pmc/articles/PMC3192298/ Accessed 04 July 2021

Levine B, (2012) *A Therapist's journey to overcoming one of the world's most challenging mental disorders,* London, Hay House UK Ltd

Lipton B, (2005) *The Biology of Belief,* San Francisco, Mountain of love/Elite Books

Lipton B, (2018) *Dr. Bruce Lipton Explains how we are programmed at birth,* Available at https://www.youtube.com/watch?v=7TivZYFlbX8 Accessed 01 October 2019

Marks T, (2019) *8 self-defeating Havocs that wreak havoc,* Available at https://www.youtube.com/watch?v=QlDXDLA4qpc Accessed 06 December 2019

McKeon P, (2018) *Bipolar Moods Treatment and Preventing Relapses,* Available at https://www.youtube.com/watch?v=FLGTxug41Uo, Accessed November 25 2019

Murtagh A, (2020) *Depression in bipolar affective disorder*, Available at https://www.medicalindependent.ie/depression-in-bipolar-affective-disorder/, Accessed July 04 2021

Nippoldt T, (2020) *Thyroid Disease: Can it affect a person's mood?* Available at https://www.mayoclinic.org/diseases-conditions/hyperthyroidism/expert-answers/thyroid-disease/faq-20058228 Accessed 01 July 2021

O'Carroll S, (2013), *Delays of 10 years in diagnosis of bipolar disorder*, Available at https://www.thejournal.ie/delays-of-up-to-10-years-in-diagnosing-bipolar-disorder-902005-May2013/, Accessed 15 June 2019

Parker G, (2019), *Bipolar II Disorder: Modelling, Measuring and Managing* (Third Edition), Sydney, Cambridge University Press

Preston J, Fast J (2006), *Take charge of bipolar disorder*, New York, Grand Central Publishing.

Reid, I. (2012), *Stephen Fry the Secret Life of the Manic Depressive part two*, https://www.youtube.com/watch?v=B3rHTm1YLxA&t=121s, Accessed November 20 2019

Purse M, (2019) *Grandiosity in Bipolar Disorder*, Available at https://www.verywellmind.com/grandiosity-in-bipolar-disorder-definition-and-stories-378818, Accessed 16 November 2019

Purse M, (2019) *Pressured Speech in Bipolar Disorder*, Available at: https://www.verywellmind.com/what-is-pressured-speech-378822, Accessed 05 September 2019

Runko V, (2009) *Cognitive Behavioural Therapy for Insomnia (CBT-1)*, Washington, The Ross Centre for Anxiety and Related Disorders

Smith I, (2015) *Managing bipolar without medication*, Available at http://theconversation.com/managing-bipolar-disorder-without-medication-48640, Accessed 01 August 2019

Star K, (2019) *Mental Filters and Panic Disorder*, Available at https://www.verywellmind.com/mental-filters-and-panic-disorder-2584186 accessed 01062019

Waite J, Easton A (2013) *The ECT Handbook* 3rd Edition, London, RC Psych Publications

Warin C, (2016) *Understanding Hypomania and Mania*, London, Mind 2016

World Health Organization (2016), *Mental Health and Substance Abuse: Suicide Data, 01 February.* Available at *https://www.who.int/mental_health/prevention/suicide/suicideprevent/en/* Accessed 08 March 2020

Weingus L, (2019) *Struggling with depression? Here's how journaling can help.* Available at https://www.mindbodygreen.com/articles/how-journaling-can-help-with-depression Accessed 04 July 2021

White A, (2020*) Can You Have Bipolar Disorder and an anxiety disorder at the Same Time?* Available at https://www.healthline.com/health/bipolar-and-anxiety Accessed 04 July 2021

Printed in Great Britain
by Amazon